MONETARY POLICY AND PRICE STABILITY

MARC LABONTE
AND
GAIL MAKINEN

Novinka Books
An imprint of Nova Science Publishers, Inc.
New York

For permission to use material from this book please contact us:
Telephone 631-231-7269; Fax 631-231-8175
Web Site: http://www.novapublishers.com

Library of Congress Cataloging-in-Publication Data:
Labonte, Marc.
Monetary policy and price stability / Marc Labonte and Gail Makinen.
p. cm.
Includes index.
ISBN 1-59454-890-0
1. Monetary policy--United States. 2. Money supply--United States. 3. Fiscal policy--United States. 4. Prices--Government policy--United States. 5. Board of Governors of the Federal Reserve System (U.S.) I. Makinen, Gail E. II. Title.
HG540.L33 2004
339.5'3--dc22 2005033098

Published by Nova Science Publishers, Inc. ✢ New York

MONETARY POLICY AND PRICE STABILITY

CONTENTS

PREFACE

Monetary policy can be defined broadly as any policy relating to the supply of money. Since the main agency concerned with the supply of money is the nation's central bank, the Federal Reserve, monetary policy can also be defined in terms of the directives, policies, statements, and actions of the Federal Reserve, particularly those from its Board of Governors that have an effect on aggregate demand or national spending. The nation's financial press and markets pay particular attention to the pronouncements of the chairman of the Board of Governors, the nation's central banker.

The reason for this attention is that monetary policy can have important effects on aggregate demand and through it on real Gross Domestic Product (GDP), unemployment, real foreign exchange rates, real interest rates, the composition of output, etc. It is paradoxical, however, that these important effects, to the extent that they occur, are essentially only short-run in nature. Over the longer run, the major effect of monetary policy is on the rate of inflation.

Thus, while a more rapid rate of money growth may for a time stimulate the economy leading to a more rapid rate of real GDP growth and a lower unemployment rate, over the longer run these changes are undone and the economy is left with a higher rate of inflation. In some societies where high rates of inflation are endemic, more rapid rates of money growth fail to exercise any stimulating effect and are almost immediately translated into higher rates of inflation.

Traditionally, two means have been used to measure the posture of monetary policy. Since monetary policy involves the Federal Reserve's contribution to aggregate demand or money spending, it would be logical to examine the growth rate of the money supply. A growing money supply is important for the subsequent growth in money spending or aggregate demand. Giving empirical content to the abstract concept of "the supply of money" has not been easy. For the United States, three different collections of assets have been defined as "money" and labeled M1, M2, and M3.

Unfortunately, over the period 1990-2004 these aggregates have not been consistently linked to money spending and, consequently, they are not the major focus of monetary policy. Rather, the Federal Reserve executes monetary policy by setting a target for an overnight interest rate called the federal funds rate. Low or falling rates are usually taken as a sign of monetary ease; high or rising rates usually indicate monetary tightness. Changes in the federal funds rates affect primarily short-term interest rates, and through these changes, money spending.

The book then looks more closely at five economies that have adopted a price stability goal: New Zealand (which was the first country to adopt targeting), Canada, the United Kingdom, Sweden, and the euro area. One key finding from these case studies is that, in practice, central banks tend to operate with greater latitude and more discretion than some targeting proponents may have envisioned. For example, central banks still tend to respond to a decline in economic activity by lowering interest rates, even though strict attention to the target might not justify it.

This is possible because exceptions to the targets are granted for a variety of shocks and the definition of inflation being targeted often excludes price changes due to factors such as food, energy, and excise taxes.

The book concludes with a brief analysis of the record of inflation targeting in the developing world. It finds that the improvement in economic performance following the adoption of inflation targeting is greater in the developing world. Since developing world countries often experience economic and political instability.

Chapter 1

MONETARY POLICY: CURRENT POLICY AND CONDITIONS*

SUMMARY

Monetary policy can be defined broadly as any policy relating to the supply of money. Since the main agency concerned with the supply of money is the nation's central bank, the Federal Reserve, monetary policy can also be defined in terms of the directives, policies, statements, and actions of the Federal Reserve, particularly those from its Board of Governors that have an effect on aggregate demand or national spending. The nation's financial press and markets pay particular attention to the pronouncements of the chairman of the Board of Governors, the nation's central banker. The reason for this attention is that monetary policy can have important effects on aggregate demand and through it on real Gross Domestic Product (GDP), unemployment, real foreign exchange rates, real interest rates, the composition of output, etc.

It is paradoxical, however, that these important effects, to the extent that they occur, are essentially only short-run in nature. Over the longer run, the major effect of monetary policy is on the rate of inflation. Thus, while a more rapid rate of money growth may for a time stimulate the economy leading to a more rapid rate of real GDP growth and a lower unemployment rate, over the longer run these changes are undone and the economy is left with a higher rate of inflation. In some societies where high rates of inflation are endemic,

---

* Excerpted from CRS Report RL30354, dated June 20, 2005.

more rapid rates of money growth fail to exercise any stimulating effect and are almost immediately translated into higher rates of inflation.

Traditionally, two means have been used to measure the posture of monetary policy. Since monetary policy involves the Federal Reserve's contribution to aggregate demand or money spending, it would be logical to examine the growth rate of the money supply. A growing money supply is important for the subsequent growth in money spending or aggregate demand. Giving empirical content to the abstract concept of "the supply of money" has not been easy. For the United States, three different collections of assets have been defined as "money" and labeled M1, M2, and M3. Unfortunately, over the period 1990-2004 these aggregates have not been consistently linked to money spending and, consequently, they are not the major focus of monetary policy.

Rather, the Federal Reserve executes monetary policy by setting a target for an overnight interest rate called the federal funds rate. Low or falling rates are usually taken as a sign of monetary ease; high or rising rates usually indicate monetary tightness. Changes in the federal funds rates affect primarily short-term interest rates, and through these changes, money spending.

Between January 3, 2001, and June 25, 2003, the target rate for federal funds was reduced to 1.0% from 6-1/2%. This policy was reversed beginning June 30, 2004. In eight equal increments of 1/4% ending on May 3, 2005, the target rate was raised to 3% from 1%.

The behavior of the U.S. economy is affected significantly by the behavior of monetary policy. And monetary policy over the past three years has been expansionary. Monetary policy changes typically affect the economy with a 12-18-month lag.

The 1991-2001 economic expansion, the longest in American history, came to an end in March 2001. Economic growth became sluggish during the second half of 2000 and remained sluggish through 2001. During that year GDP contracted during the first three quarters. Positive growth resumed in the fourth quarter and has continued throughout 2002 and 2003. Prior to mid-2000, the economy was growing at a rate that was thought to be unsustainable. To curb growth, the Federal Reserve between mid-1999 and May 2000 raised the target for the federal funds rate to 6-1/2% from 4-3/4%. Apparently this tightening of monetary policy was too severe, for economic growth collapsed soon thereafter. In the presence of slumping economic growth, falling industrial production, and an increasing unemployment rate, the Federal Reserve began aggressively easing monetary policy. Between

January 3 and December 11, 2001, the target for the federal funds rate was reduced to 1-3/4% from 6-1/2%. Short-term interest rates have generally followed the decline in the target for the federal funds rate. Longer-term rates, however, have proven to be more resilient and have not fallen as much. On November 6, 2002, the Fed reduced the target to 1-1/4% from 1-3/4%. On June 25, 2003, the target federal funds rate was lowered to1.0%. In a move toward tightening monetary policy, the target rate was increased by 1/4% on June 30, August 10, September 21, November 10, and December 14, 2004, and February 2, March 22, and May 3, 2005, and now stands at 3%.

The growth rates of the various measures of money have been quite different and do not necessarily provide much information on the various shifts in monetary policy. Several measures, such as aggregate reserves and M1, have been contracting over some recent years while others, such as M2 and M3, have grown at positive but highly variable rates over the same time period. The only measure that has enjoyed a fairly consistent rate of growth is the monetary base, and this aggregate is composed largely of circulating paper currency, much of which appears to be abroad and is not necessarily related to economic conditions in the United States.

WHAT IS MONETARY POLICY?

Broadly speaking, monetary policy is any policy related to the supply of money. As such, it would encompass various activities of the U.S. Treasury for those relating to foreign exchange operations and the receipt and disposition of public funds can affect the supply of money. The dominant influence on the U.S. money supply, however, comes from the policies of the nation's central bank, the Federal Reserve, and particularly those policies originating with its Board of Governors. Thus, a more realistic definition of monetary policy would be that it consists of the directives, policies, pronouncements, and actions of the Federal Reserve that affect aggregate demand or national spending. Among these, the dominant action consists of open market operations. These involve the buying and selling of seasoned Treasury securities by the Federal Reserve. When Treasury securities are purchased, the Federal Reserve does so with newly created money. This money can serve as reserves for the financial system and allows commercial banks and other depository institutions to make new loans and investments, thereby expanding the money supply and aggregate demand. The opposite happens when the Federal Reserve sells government securities.

IS MONETARY POLICY IMPORTANT?

It has been said that "money matters" and the case for this statement can be made in at least two different contexts. In one, monetary policy is compared with fiscal policy and, given the current international financial system with flexible exchange rates and a high degree of capital mobility between countries, the ability of changes in the money supply to affect aggregate demand and the pace of GDP growth and employment is great compared with fiscal policy. In the other context, changes in the money supply have the potential to bring about major changes in the growth of GDP and employment only in the *short run*. Paradoxically, this is not true over the *longer run*. Over the more extended horizon, money supply growth has its primary effect only on the rate of inflation. How fast GDP grows or what the unemployment rate is, is largely independent of the amount of money or its growth rate. A brief discussion of each of the two contexts summarized above follows.

Monetary vs. Fiscal Policy

The standard macroeconomic model makes a compelling case for the relative importance of monetary policy in a world whose financial arrangements involve the use of flexible exchange rates and where capital is highly mobile between countries. To see this, fiscal and monetary expansion will be contrasted.

Let us allow the full employment budget deficit to rise (or the full-employment surplus to fall) through either a tax rate cut or a rise in appropriated expenditures. While the increase in this budget deficit (or fall in surplus) raises aggregate demand, it also raises the borrowing requirement of the government (or lowers the amount of debt it retires) and its demand for funds in financial markets. This then causes domestic interest rates to rise relative to those in other financial centers. The rise in domestic interest rates makes U.S. financial assets more attractive to foreigners. They, in turn, increase the demand for dollars in foreign exchange markets to acquire the wherewithal to purchase U.S. assets. The increased demand for dollars causes the dollar to appreciate. Dollar appreciation then reduces the cost of foreign goods and services to Americans and raises the price of American goods and services to foreigners. As a result, U.S. spending on imports tends to rise and foreign spending on U.S. exports tends to fall. Thus, any expansionary effects on domestic demand from the larger budget deficit tends to be offset in part or total by a reduced foreign trade surplus or a larger foreign trade deficit.[1]

A more expansive monetary policy centering on a more rapid rate of growth of the money supply initially serves to lower U.S. interest rates relative to those in other financial centers. Foreign financial assets become more attractive to U.S. investors, the supply of dollars to the foreign exchange markets rises as U.S. investors attempt to acquire foreign currencies to buy foreign assets, and the dollar depreciates. Dollar depreciation then makes foreign goods and services more expensive to Americans and American goods and services cheaper to foreigners. As a result, the United States spends less on imports and foreigners spend more on U.S. exports. A falling foreign trade deficit or rising trade surplus thus reinforces any stimulus to domestic demand that comes from lower U.S. interest rates.

The implication from the standard macroeconomic model is that monetary expansion is far more powerful than fiscal policy in influencing GDP growth and employment.

Short Run vs. Longer Run

The analysis above quite clearly shows that a more rapid rate of growth of the money supply can cause domestic demand to expand. An examination of U.S. economic history will show that money-induced demand expansions can have a positive effect on U.S. GDP growth and total employment. This same evidence, however, also suggests that over the longer run, a more rapid rate of growth of the money supply is largely dissipated in a more rapid rate of inflation with little if any lasting effect on real GDP and employment.

Economists have two explanations for this paradoxical behavior. First, they note that, in the short run, many economies have an elaborate system of contracts (both implicit and explicit) that makes it difficult in a short period for significant adjustments to take place in wages and prices in response to more rapid money growth. Second, they note that expectations for one reason or another are slow to adjust to the longer run consequences of major changes in monetary policy. This slow adjustment also adds rigidities to wages and prices. Because of these rigidities, changes in money supply growth that change aggregate demand can have a large initial effect on output and employment. Over the longer run, as contracts are renegotiated and expectations adjust, wages and prices rise in response to the change in demand and much of the change in output and employment is undone. Thus, money can matter in the short run but be fairly neutral for GDP growth and employment in the longer run.

It is noteworthy that in societies where high rates of inflation are endemic, the short run may be very short indeed. During the final stages of very rapid inflations, called hyperinflation, money's ability to alter GDP growth and employment is virtually nonexistent.

INDICATORS OF MONETARY POLICY

It is common to speak of monetary policy as being "easy" or being "tight" or even of being "neutral." What exactly do these terms mean and how does one measure the posture of monetary policy?

Two basic measures of the posture of monetary policy are frequently used: the growth rate of the money supply and market interest rates, particularly the federal funds rate (the interest rate that one bank charges another for reserves that are lent on an overnight basis). Unfortunately, as the following discussion makes clear, neither of these two indicators provides an unambiguous measure of the posture of monetary policy.

MONEY SUPPLY GROWTH

Because the growth in aggregate demand depends heavily on the growth in the supply of money, it would be logical to measure the posture of monetary policy by the growth rate of the supply of money. Using this indicator, monetary policy is said to be *easy* when, during a sustained period, the supply of money increases at a rate that is high or rising relative to a recent trend. Alternatively, policy is said to be *tight* when the rate of money growth is low or falling relative to a trend.

To measure the posture of monetary policy, the abstract concept "the supply of money" must be given an empirical content. That is, the supply of money must be defined in terms of an asset or group of assets that can be measured. Moreover, that asset or group of assets must be stably or predictably related to aggregate demand or money spending. The latter condition is important. It means that, when the supply of money is changed, it will be possible to predict its effect on money spending.

In the United States, we do not have a unique asset or group of assets that the Federal Reserve defines as money. Rather, three collections of assets are recognized as money and are designated as M1, M2, and M3 (for a definition of each, see the appendix). They are constructed such that M3 includes M2, and M2 includes M1. It is possible for the growth of one or two of the aggregates to rise or fall when the growth of the other aggregate or aggregates falls or rises (a common reason for this is that wealth owners can shift dollars from one type of account to another such as when they shift from passbook savings, an account included in M2 but not M1, into checking accounts on which interest is paid, an account included in both M1 and M2). When these divergent movements take place, as they have over much of the past 12 years in the United States (see Table 2), how is one to characterize monetary policy?

A simple way to answer this question is to see which aggregate best explains the subsequent movements in aggregate demand. During much of the post-World War II period, M1 had the most stable relationship to aggregate demand. Nevertheless, the Federal Reserve, beginning in the 1970s, set target growth rate ranges for all three aggregates. Unfortunately, during the late 1970s, the stable relationship between M1 and aggregate spending broke down and the Federal Reserve, while still reporting movements in this aggregate, no longer sets growth rate ranges for it. During the 1990s, the stable relationship between M2 and aggregate spending also broke down. Beginning in July 2000, the Fed discontinued setting monitoring ranges for M2 and M3. Legislation requiring it to do so expired. (While M3 was never strongly related to aggregate demand, its movement also bore little relationship to subsequent movements in demand during the 1990s.)

Thus, the United States now has three definitions of money that appear to provide little information about the posture of monetary policy. Moreover, an extensive amount of recent research on the stability issue has yet to yield a collection of new assets that performs consistently better, that is, provide consistently superior information on the posture of monetary policy.[2]

Interest Rates

A logical reason for focusing on interest rates in judging monetary policy is that they are an important link by which changes in the money supply are transmitted to the real economy. That is, changes in money supply growth lead to changes in market interest rates and these changes then influence households in their decisions to buy homes, automobiles, appliances, and the like, and businesses in their decisions regarding inventories and plant and equipment purchases.[3]

The interest rate relevant for these decisions is not the market rate but the real rate or market rate less the expected rate of inflation. Rising real rates are interpreted as a sign of tight monetary policy while falling real rates supposedly signal a move toward an easier monetary policy. Caution should be used, however, in making this interpretation of the movement in real rates. The reason is that market interest rates respond both to shifts in the supply and demand for money.[4]

Those who use interest rates as guides to the posture of monetary policy appear to implicitly assume that shifts in the supply of money dominate movements in the relevant interest rates. Thus, a more rapid rate of growth of the money supply should drive down market interest rates, especially short-term rates. Given expectations about future inflation, the fall in market rates is taken as a fall in real rates and a signal that monetary policy has eased; and, conversely, for a rise in market and real rates.

Market interest rates, however, can fall for two other reasons even when the supply of money (or its growth rate) is held constant. First, any fall in income reduces the demand for money and, as a result, market interest rates and real rates will fall. Second, should the public come to expect a lower inflation rate, inflation expectations should also fall. With this decline, market interest rates should also fall. However, real interest rates should not fall and may even rise in the short run. Thus, the fall in market rates should not stimulate economic activity.

An important interest rate for the Federal Reserve is the federal funds rate, which is essentially an overnight rate that one depository institution charges another when reserves are lent — reserves being necessary to back the deposit liabilities financial institutions have on their books. If the Federal Reserve wishes to expand the reserves of depository institutions thereby enhancing their lending capabilities, it will supply reserves to this market. The increased supply will drive down the federal funds rate and monetary policy can be said to have eased.

Conversely, when the Federal Reserve wishes to tighten lending, it will withdraw reserves from this market causing the funds rate to rise. Thus, a falling funds rate is often taken to signal an easing of monetary policy, a rising rate the tightening of policy, and a constant rate, a neutral or "stand fast" policy. However, this is not always the case and each movement can have unintended consequences.

This arises because the Federal Reserve, through the federal funds rate, only controls the supply of reserves. It does not control the demand for reserves. That is in the domain of financial institutions and is governed by their outlook for economic activity. A constant federal funds rate, for example, may not be a neutral policy. Suppose that financial institutions become pessimistic about the future and cut back their demand for reserves. Reserve growth declines as does lending and economic activity. During the period these advents are transpiring, the Federal Reserve keeps the funds rate constant. The effect on the economy is not neutral.

How long this would continue before it became apparent to the Federal Reserve that the economy had shifted is open to conjecture. After some period of time, data would reveal the falloff in the growth of the reserves of depository institutions and the monetary aggregates. Misinterpretations such as this are most costly when an economy is at a critical turning point.

THE RECENT AND CURRENT POSTURE OF MONETARY POLICY

The behavior of several important performance characteristics of the U.S. economy since the early 1980s is shown in Table 1. Of concern is the period of GDP growth from 1994 to 2000. Rates of from 4% to 5% were regarded as unsustainable. These rates played an important role in causing the Federal Reserve to tighten monetary policy.

Monetary policy played an important role in bringing to an end the longest economic expansion in U.S. history (March 1991 to March 2000) as well as setting in motion the current expansion. As noted above there are two ways to measure the posture of monetary policy: the growth of the monetary aggregates and interest rates.

The behavior of the aggregates is shown in Table 2. The first impression is that they do not tell a consistent story. Aggregate Reserves and to a lesser degree M1 have contracted over most of 1994-2002 while the Monetary Base, M2, and M3 grew positively in each year (a definition of each aggregate is given in the appendix). All is, however, not what it seems. The decline in Aggregate Reserves actually allowed for considerable monetary expansion. This occurs because individuals and businesses allowed their demand deposit balances to run off (see Table 3). This decline in demand deposit balances has set free bank reserves. Since not all of these reserves were removed from the banking system, reserve contraction is compatible with expanding the lending capacity of banks. (The increase in aggregate reserves in 2001 was temporary and designed to forestall a possible liquidity crisis in the immediate aftermath of the September 11 terrorist attacks.)

Table 1. Recent Economic Performance

Year	Real Growth[a]	Inflation Rate[b]	Unemployment Rate
1983	7.7	3.4	9.6
1984	5.6	3.6	7.5
1985	4.2	2.8	7.2
1986	2.8	2.4	7.0
1987	4.5	2.8	6.2
1988	3.7	3.8	5.5
1989	2.7	3.4	5.3
1990	0.7	4.1	5.6
1991	1.1	3.0	6.8
1992	4.1	2.2	7.5
1993	2.5	2.3	6.9
1994	4.1	2.2	6.1[c]
1995	2.0	2.0	5.6
1996	4.4	1.9	5.4
1997	4.3	1.5	4.9
1998	4.5	1.1	4.5
1999	4.7	1.6	4.2
2000	2.2	2.2	4.0
2001	0.0	2.4	4.7
2002	2.8	1.4	5.8
2003	4.3	1.5	6.0
2004	3.9	2.4	5.5
2005	3.5	3.1	5.2

Source: U.S. Departments of Labor and Commerce.

a. Real growth and inflation are measured on a fourth quarter over fourth quarter basis. 2005 data are for the first quarter. For unemployment, the average over the first 5-months of 2005. b. Inflation measured by the implicit price deflator for GDP. c. The unemployment rates beginning in 1994 are based on a revised questionnaire and are not strictly comparable with those of previous years. All years are annual averages.

The behavior of the Monetary Base could account for both the recovery that began in the fourth quarter of 2001 and the subsequent expansion of the economy. However, this may be due to chance since approximately 90% of the Base consists of paper currency (and coin) in circulation, much of which apparently does not circulate within the United States.[5] Thus, its behavior may depend on conditions in foreign countries rather than reflect economic developments in the United States.

Table 2. The Growth Rates of the Monetary Aggregates (annualized rates of change)

Time Period	Aggregate Reserves	Monetary Base	M1	M2	M3
90:12-91:12	9.0	8.3	8.7	3.0	1.3
91:12-92:12	19.6	10.5	14.3	1.6	0.3
92:12-93:12	11.3	10.5	10.3	1.6	1.4
93:12-94:12	1.8	8.2	1.8	0.4	1.7
94:12-95:12	5.0	3.9	2.0	4.1	6.0
95:12-96:12	-11.2	4.0	4.1	4.7	7.3
96:12-97:12	6.6	6.1	0.7	5.7	9.1
97:12-98:12	-3.5	7.0	2.2	8.8	11.0
98:12-99:12	-7.6	15.3	2.3	6.0	8.3
99:12-00:12	-7.3	-1.5	-3.0	6.2	8.6
00:12-01:12	6.7	8.7	8.3	10.5	12.9
01:12-02:12	-2.8	7.2	3.2	6.4	6.5
02:12-03:12	6.9	5.7	6.2	4.6	3.3
03:12-04:12	8.8	5.4	5.4	5.5	6.1
04:05-05:05	0.6	4.6	2.7	3.2	4.3

Source: Board of Governors of the Federal Reserve System.

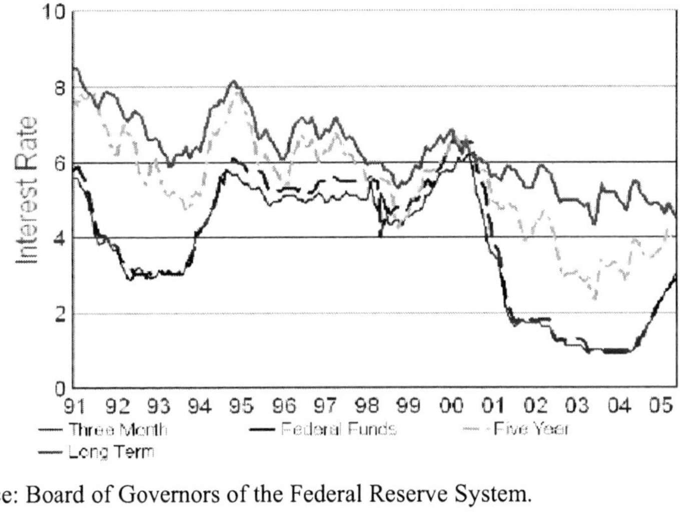

Source: Board of Governors of the Federal Reserve System.

Figure 1. Yield on Selected Securities and Federal Funds (%)

Alternatively, while the behavior of M1 could account for the beginning of the expansion, it would have some difficulty accounting for its continuation. Conversely, the behavior of M2 and M3 might explain both the initiation and continuation of the current recovery.

A general conclusion from the behavior of the aggregates is that, while they might yield some useful information about the economic expansion, they do not provide consistent information on the posture of monetary policy since it is well known that they are not used by the Federal Reserve to manipulate the growth in aggregate demand. Rather, the behavior of the Federal Reserve and the posture of monetary policy is best inferred from interest rates, particularly the behavior of the federal funds rate.

The movement of selected U.S. Treasury yields and the federal funds rate is shown in Figure 1. The sharp decline in the rate that began in late 1990 played a major role in initiating the cyclical upswing that began in March 1991. As the expansion began to take hold, the Federal Reserve kept the rate target constant at about 3% from late 1992 through early 1994. As momentum built and the economy moved toward full employment, the rate was raised to slow growth. The increase appeared to be too large as GDP growth slowed to about 2.3% in 1995. In three small adjustment, the last on January 31, 1996, the federal funds rate target was lowered to 5-1/4%. The growth rate of GDP during 1996 was above the rate the Federal Reserve thought to be sustainable. As a result, the federal funds rate target was hiked to 5-1/2% on March 25, 1997. However, beginning in the second quarter of 1998, GDP growth slowed significantly. To boost demand growth as well as provide support to ease the Asian and Russian financial crises, the Federal Reserve reduced the funds rate target by 1/4% on September 29, October 15, and November 17, 1998, for a total reduction of 3/4%. As the crisis conditions eased, the Federal Reserve hiked the rate target by 1/4% in June, August, and November of 1999. To slow GDP growth to a more sustainable rate, the federal funds rate target was hiked on February 2, March 21, and May 16, 2000. The final increase brought the rate to 6-1/2%. It appears that these increases had too severe an effect on GDP growth, for the rate target was reduced to 6% on January 3, 2001. Between then and August 21, the rate was reduced six more times to 3-1/2% from 6%. On September 17, to avert a possible liquidity crisis following the terrorist attacks of September 11, the rate was reduced to 3.0%. In a follow-up action, the rate was reduced three more times and on December 11, it stood at 1-3/4%. The target rate was reduced once in 2002 (November 6) and once in 2003 (June 25) when it reached a low of 1.0%. As growth gathered momentum, the unemployment rate fell, and the inflation rate moved upward, the Fed tightened policy, increasing the target in eight equal increments of 1/4% beginning June 30, 2004, and ending May 3, 2005. The target rate now stands at 3%.

Note that, while short-term interest rates move in sympathy with the federal funds rate, longer-term rates often do not. The divergence is especially noticeable during 1996, 1997, 1999, and 2001 to 2004. This should help dispel the notion that the Federal Reserve can set interest rates wherever it wishes.

Table 3. Growth in Major Components of M2 (annualized rates of change)

Time Period	Currency	Demand Deposits	Other Checking Deposits	Nontransactions Component[a]
90:12-91:12	8.3	4.4	13.2	1.2
91:12-92:12	9.3	17.4	16.8	-3.0
92:12-93:12	10.1	13.4	7.9	-2.1
93:12-94:12	10.0	-0.5	-2.5	-0.2
94:12-95:12	5.1	1.5	-11.8	7.1
95:12-96:12	5.9	3.4	-22.6	8.7
96:12-97:12	7.7	-1.7	11.0	8.2
97:12-98:12	8.2	-4.1	1.8	11.2
98:12-99:12	12.2	-6.2	-2.5	6.9
99:12-01:12	2.4	-11.9	-1.6	9.2
00:12-01:12	9.5	6.3	8.4	11.2
01:12-02:12	7.8	-9.0	8.2	7.5
02:12-03:12	5.8	3.5	11.2	4.1
03:12-04:12	5.3	5.5	5.6	5.6
04:05-05:05	4.8	-0.3	1.4	3.3

Source: Board of Governors of the Federal Reserve System. a. Consists principally of savings accounts (including money market deposit accounts) and time certificates of deposits.

THE FEDERAL RESERVE AND THE MONETARY AGGREGATES

In its report to the Congress, dated July 20, 1993, the Board of Governors expressed considerable uncertainty about the usefulness of M2 and M3 as measures of money. The uncertainty arose from the perverse movement in the velocity or turnover rates of these aggregates during the previous three years.

For this reason, the Board of Governors decided to de-emphasize both M2 and M3 in its decision-making. While the board continued to set growth rate ranges for each aggregate, it concluded:

> With considerable uncertainty persisting about the relationship of the monetary aggregates to spending, the behavior of the aggregates relative to their annual ranges will likely be of limited use in guiding policy... and the Federal Reserve will continue to utilize a broad range of financial and economic indicators in assessing its policy stance.

This position was reaffirmed by the board during subsequent Humphrey-Hawkins hearings. However, in the Monetary Policy Report submitted to Congress on July 20, 2000, the Board of Governors stated:

> At its June meeting, the FOMC did not establish ranges for the growth of money and debt in 2000 and 2001. The legal requirement to establish and to announce such ranges had expired, and owing to uncertainties about the behavior of the velocities of debt and money, these ranges for many years have not provided useful benchmarks for the conduct of monetary policy. Nevertheless, the FOMC believes that the behavior of money and credit will continue to have value for gauging economic and financial conditions. . . .

THE NEAR-TERM GOALS OF MONETARY POLICY

In its semi-annual *Monetary Policy Report to the Congress*, dated February 16, 2005, the Board of Governors of the Federal Reserve presented its economic projections for 2005 and 2006. It projected the growth of real GDP during this year to be between 3.5% and 4.0% (measured on a fourth-quarter over fourth-quarter basis). The unemployment rate is projected to average between 5.0% and 5.5% during the fourth quarter and the Personal Consumption Expenditure price index, less food and energy, from the GDP accounts is expected to rise from 1.5% to 2.0%, also over the four quarters of the year.[6] For 2006, the relevant projections are 3.25% to 3.75% for GDP, 1.5% to 2.0% for prices, and 5.0% to 5.25% for the unemployment rate (in the fourth quarter of the year).

APPENDIX

Definitions

M1 is the sum of the following:

1. Currency held by the public
2. Outstanding traveler's checks of nonbank issuers
3. Demand deposit balances
4. Negotiable Order of Withdrawal (NOW and Super-NOW) accounts and other checkable deposits.

M2 is the sum of the following:

1. M1
2. Time and savings deposits in amounts under $100,000
3. Individual holdings in money market mutual funds
4. Money market deposit accounts (MMDAs).

M3 is the sum of the following:

1. M2
2. Time deposits at commercial banks in amounts of $100,000 or more
3. Term repurchase agreements
4. Institution-only money market mutual funds
5. Term Eurodollars held by U.S. residents in Canada and the U.K.
6. Overnight retail purchase agreements (Repos)
7. Overnight Eurodollars held by U.S. residents.

Nonfinancial debt is the sum of the following sectors' outstanding debt:

1. U.S. government
2. State and local governments
3. Nonfinancial domestic businesses
4. Households.

REFERENCES

[1] It is important to note that this explanation requires the *full employment or structural* budget deficit to rise. Budget deficits

produced by a fall in income, or *cyclical* deficits need not produce these results.

[2] For a discussion of these studies and the issues involved, see CRS Report RL31416, *Monetary Aggregates: Their Use in the Conduct of Monetary Policy*, by Marc Labonte and Gail E. Makinen.

[3] The mechanism by which monetary policy affects money spending is contentions.

[4] The real rate of interest is determined by the interaction of saving and investment. Thus, change in the national saving rate or the desire to invest can affect the real rate independent of anything the Federal Reserve does. Such changes to the real rate can further complicate the use of interest rates as an indicator of the posture of monetary policy.

[5] For a detailed discussion, see CRS Report RL30904, *Why is the Amount of Currency in Circulation Rising?*, by Gail Makinen.

[6] The Federal Reserve substituted the price index for the personal consumption portion of GDP for the frequently used Consumer Price Index because it believes the CPI gives a greater upward bias to the inflation rate than does the price index for personal consumption.

Chapter 2

PRICE STABILITY AS THE SOLE GOAL OF MONETARY POLICY: THE INTERNATIONAL EXPERIENCE*

SUMMARY

In the 1970s, many countries were plagued by persistently high inflation rates, which were thought to cause a significant loss in economic efficiency. Since persistent inflation is considered to be ultimately the result of monetary policy, many countries in the 1990s and 2000s sought institutional reforms to their central banks to prevent a return to the 1970s experience. A popular reform was to move from giving central banks multiple policy goals to a single mandate of price stability. The single mandate was accompanied by the introduction of an inflation target, in which central banks aim to keep inflation within a pre-defined numerical range. The logic behind these reforms was a belief among proponents that it would remove the political temptation to "pump up" the economy in the short run at the expense of long-run price stability and a belief that "fine tuning" monetary policy in response to every change in economic conditions was of little value. Some Members of Congress have expressed interest in (and introduced legislation on) adopting a price stability mandate for the Federal Reserve.

This article develops quantitative measurements to analyze the success of inflation targeting abroad by comparing both the

---

* Excerpted from CRS Report RL31702, dated June 13, 2005.

performance of targeters to non-targeters and the performance of countries before and after targeting was adopted. It finds that the economic performance of targeters improved distinctly after the adoption of an inflation target, particularly in terms of lower and less variable inflation. When compared to non-targeters, however, the success is less impressive because many non-targeters also enjoyed a strong economic performance in the 1990s. This suggests that there could be some unidentified third factor that explains the success of inflation targeters. There is little evidence supporting the theory that low inflation can be achieved only at the cost of lower and more volatile economic growth. The period of disinflation that frequently accompanied the introduction of inflation targeting, however, was often temporarily costly in terms of higher unemployment and lower growth.

The article then looks more closely at five economies that have adopted a price stability goal: New Zealand (which was the first country to adopt targeting), Canada, the United Kingdom, Sweden, and the euro area. One key finding from these case studies is that, in practice, central banks tend to operate with greater latitude and more discretion than some targeting proponents may have envisioned. For example, central banks still tend to respond to a decline in economic activity by lowering interest rates, even though strict attention to the target might not justify it. This is possible because exceptions to the targets are granted for a variety of shocks and the definition of inflation being targeted often excludes price changes due to factors such as food, energy, and excise taxes.

The chapter concludes with a brief analysis of the record of inflation targeting in the developing world. It finds that the improvement in economic performance following the adoption of inflation targeting is greater in the developing world. Since developing world countries often experience economic and political instability, this may not be surprising.

The high inflation rates that bedeviled market economies during the 1970s had a profound effect on both policymakers and economists. It convinced the former that inflation can have serious and disruptive economic and social consequences. It helped convince a skeptical economics profession that "while such influences as oil price shocks, droughts, depreciation of the dollar, or excise tax hikes may boost price indexes at one time or anther, sustained inflation requires at least the acquiescence of the central bank."[1]

The conclusion that a sustained rise in the price level is a monetary phenomenon is important, for it places responsibility for continuing inflation on the central bank. It also kindled among economists renewed interest in sorting out and accounting for the costs that inflation imposed upon a society. And it led to various policy proposals for controlling inflation. One of these involves replacing the multiple goal directive under which many cental banks operate with a directive that focuses exclusively on promoting and ensuring the achievement of "price stability."

While the United States has not replaced the current multi-goal mandate of "maximum employment, stable prices, and moderate long-term interest rates"[2] for monetary policy with a single goal of "stable prices," interest in doing so has had support from both Democratic and Republican Members of Congress. An early example of Democratic support was the "Zero Inflation Resolution" introduced by Congressman Stephen Neal of North Carolina in 1989. In the 109th Congress, Representative Jim Saxton, Republican of New Jersey, introduced the Price Stability Act of 2005, H.R. 498, which would mandate price stability as the primary goal of the monetary policy of the Board of Governors of the Federal Reserve System and the Federal Open Market Committee.

A goal of "price stability" has become the focus of monetary policy in most industrialized countries and a number of developing countries. Typically, this goal has been carried out by giving central banks an inflation target to meet (or the central banks have given themselves such a target). The experience of four of them, New Zealand, Canada, the United Kingdom, and Sweden, whose central banks have either been directed or chosen to focus on such a goal, will be reviewed here in some detail. In addition, the chapter will review the European Central Bank (ECB), which has operated monetary policy since 1999 under a single goal of price stability for the euro area, an economy whose GDP is about three-quarters that of the United States.

The reason for reviewing this experience is straightforward. The proposal for a single goal of price stability has been controversial, both politically and within the economics profession, with proponents claiming that it would promote low inflation and macroeconomic stability and opponents claiming that low inflation would come at the expense of macroeconomic stability. Furthermore, while implementing a directive to achieve and maintain price stability sounds simple, it can involve many technical problems such as how to define the goal; which price index to use in measuring price stability; what exceptions, if any, to permit; whether the target should be a range or a point; who should set the target; the period for which it should be set; what type of accountability should be enforced; and so on.[3] The experience of these countries in implementing and operating monetary policy under a single goal to promote "price stability" should be of value to U.S. policymakers, for it can provide insight into problems that might be encountered in implementing such a strategy, as well as reduce uncertainty about how monetary policy functions under a single goal regime.

The Experience of Industrialized Countries that Focus Monetary Policy on a Goal of Price Stability

Monetary policy has two main goals. First, it seeks to provide price stability, in terms of a low and stable rate of inflation. Second, it seeks to provide economic stability. While it is a long standing view among economists that manipulating the money supply cannot influence the long run growth rate of an economy, it can mitigate the booms and busts of the business cycle in the short run. These goals will sometimes conflict, but are often compatible.[4]

Given these two goals, it may seem strange that many central banks now focus monetary policy on a single goal of price stability. But how to best pursue the second goal, economic stability, is a matter of some controversy. Proponents of inflation targeting claim that a single goal regime would lead to lower inflation and a more stable business cycle. This claim is based on an argument that is both political and economic in nature. They argue that when central banks are not given clear policy goals, they are vulnerable to political pressures to use expansionary monetary policy to boost economic growth above its sustainable rate for short-term political gain. The long run consequences of such an opportunistic policy, they argue, is higher inflation and a monetary policy that over time is less effective at altering aggregate demand. By holding central banks to a sole goal of price stability, proponents claim that monetary policy can no longer be abused for political purposes. By preventing abuse, the sole goal of price stability becomes compatible with the other goal, economic stability. Furthermore, these proponents are likely to be influenced by a body of literature that suggests that when central bankers "fine tune" monetary policy to stabilize the economy, they are likely to do more harm than good because of the time lags and uncertainty inherent in monetary policy.[5] Focusing on price stability, they argue, gives central bankers a long-term perspective that is more appropriate.

Opponents of inflation targeting argue that the economic stability goal should not be officially subordinated to the price stability goal. They argue that doing so will exacerbate the booms and busts of the business cycle to society's detriment. In particular, they fear that too great a focus on low inflation will lead to needlessly sluggish growth and high unemployment. They argue that it is possible for monetary policy to pursue both goals responsibly. They point to the economy's complexity and the multitude of potential shocks that could affect an economy as rationales for giving central bankers as much discretionary decision-making power as possible.

Both sides make compelling arguments, and since the arguments are partly political, they cannot be settled by theory alone. To an extent, the argument can be settled empirically, however. Both sides claim that their policies would lead to (or at least not prevent) low and stable inflation and stable economic growth. Since so many foreign central banks operate under an inflation target, one can look to international experience to see which argument receives the most support.

The question can be answered in two ways. First, did countries that adopted inflation targets have lower and stabler inflation and more stable growth after the adoption of the target? Second, did inflation targeters have lower and stabler inflation and more stable growth than non-targeters? These are useful questions because even if a country saw its macroeconomic performance improve after the adoption of an inflation target, it could be due to a broader change in the economy or the political climate. For example, macroeconomic performance could have improved because voters became less tolerant of high inflation, the economy was subject to fewer supply shocks, or policymakers' understanding of the economy improved. If the improvement were due to any of these other reasons, then the adoption of an inflation target by policymakers uncommitted to responsible policy would not lead to a decline in inflation.[6] By comparing targeters to non-targeters, one can gauge whether the improvement in a targeting country was part of a broader trend rather than the adoption of a target.[7]

Tables 1 and 2 compare the economic performance of inflation targeters and non-targeters, respectively. The average inflation rate will indicate whether inflation has been kept low, and the standard deviation of inflation over time will indicate whether it was kept stable.[8] Monetary policy cannot determine the long-run growth rate of the economy, but it can influence its stability, in terms of smoothing the ups and downs of the business cycle. The output gap and standard deviation of economic growth is used to determine if economic performance was kept stable. The output gap is a measure of how far an economy is operating from full potential (i.e., all of its resources are employed), and is measured as a percentage of GDP; using the average absolute value (so that positive and negative output gaps do not cancel each other out) is more appropriate if one assumes that it is undesirable to be above or below full potential.[9]

Table 1. Economic Performance of Inflation Targeters, Before and After (Industrialized Countries)

Country	Inflation Rate — Average	Inflation Rate — Standard Deviation	Output Gap — Average of the Absolute Value	Economic Growth — Standard Deviation
Australia				
pre-target (1985-1994)	5.3%	3.0%	1.4%	2.1%
post-target (1995-2004)	2.7%	1.5%	0.9%	0.8%
Canada				
pre-target (1982-1991)	5.3%	1.9%	1.9%	2.8%
post-target (1992-2001)	1.7%	0.7%	1.0%	1.5%
Iceland				
pre-target (1992-2001)	3.2%	1.6%	3.0%	2.7%
post-target (2002-2004)	3.3%	1.4%	1.9%	3.3%
Israel				
pre-target (1988-1997)	13.8%	4.0%	n/a	2.2%
post-target (1998-2004)	2.7%	2.6%	n/a	3.1%
New Zealand				
pre-target (1981-1990)	11.1%	7.3%	1.8%	2.3%
post-target (1991-2000)	2.1%	0.6%	2.2%	2.5%
Norway				
pre-target (1992-2001)	2.3%	0.6%	1.9%	1.4%
post-target (2002-2004)	1.4%	1.1%	0.7%	1.3%

Table 1. Continued

Country	Inflation Rate — Average	Inflation Rate — Standard Deviation	Output Gap — Average of the Absolute Value	Economic Growth — Standard Deviation
Sweden				
pre-target (1983-1992)	6.7%	2.5%	2.6%	1.9%
post-target (1993-2002)	2.0%	1.2%	2.2%	2.1%
Switzerland				
pre-target (1990-1999)	2.3%	2.0%	1.8%	1.3%
post-target (2000-2004)	0.9%	0.4%	1.0%	1.5%
United Kingdom				
pre-target (1983-1992)	5.3%	1.3%	1.1%	2.0%
post-target (1993-2002)	1.8%	0.6%	1.0%	0.8%
Euro Area				
pre-target (1989-1998)	3.1%	1.2%	1.7%	1.3%
post-target (1999-2004)	2.0%	0.5%	1.0%	1.2%

Source: CRS calculations based on data from the Organization of Economic Cooperation and Development and the International Monetary Fund.

Note: Inflation is based on the CPI. The post-target period is dated from the first full year that the target is in place. Data covers 10 years before and after (if possible) inflation targeting was in place.

One problem with the sample of non-targeters is that it is very small and not diverse. There are only two large economies in the world that do not have a single explicit or legislatively imposed price stability goal (U.S. and Japan), no medium sized economies, and a handful of small economies (GDP of less than $1 trillion).

There is a significant degree of diversity in central bank regimes among non-targeters, however.[10]

How successful a country has been at achieving price stability depends on what one considers to be the optimal rate of inflation. There is widespread agreement among economists that inflation is harmful if it is higher than a few percentage points per year or negative (i.e., deflation). Under a few percentage points, however, consensus breaks down. Some economists argue for an inflation rate of zero, stressing the harmful effects that inflation has on planning and the distortions in economic activity it creates through channels such as the tax system. Other economists argue that low but positive inflation is beneficial to an economy because it helps "grease the wheels" of the economy. These economists focus on the role of sticky prices in the economy, and argue that their presence could lead to high rates of unemployment if the inflation rate were kept at zero.[11] All economists engaged in this debate recognize measurement errors in the CPI and GDP deflator that cause inflation to be overstated. If measured inflation is, say, two percentage points higher than actual inflation, then the central bank would need to target a measured inflation rate above 2% just to avoid deflation. Thus, a positive rate of measured inflation may be necessary to keep actual prices stable.

Table 2. Economic Performance of Non-Inflation Targeters (Industrialized Countries, 1995-2004)

Country	Inflation Rate — Average	Inflation Rate — Standard Deviation	Output Gap — Average of the Absolute Value	Economic Growth — Standard Deviation
Cyprus	2.8%	0.9%	n/a	2.3%
Denmark	2.2%	0.5%	0.8%	0.9%
Hong Kong	0.9%	4.8%	n/a	4.1%
Singapore	0.9%	0.9%	N/a	4.3%
United States	2.5%	0.6%	1.2%	1.2%

Source: CRS calculations based on data from the Organization of Economic Cooperation and Development and the International Monetary Fund.
Note: Inflation is based on the CPI.

As seen in Table 1, every industrialized economy has seen its average inflation rate fall after the adoption of an inflation target, except Iceland whose inflation was already fairly low and increased only slightly. In the process, many of these countries saw their inflation rates fall from uncomfortably high levels into the range that economists prefer. However, low inflation preceded inflation targeting in Switzerland, the Euro Area, Iceland, and Norway, proving that low inflation can be achieved without inflation targeting. Furthermore, prices have been more stable after the adoption of the inflation target, as the standard deviations of their average inflation rates have also fallen in each country, except Norway which already had a stable inflation rate before the inflation target was adopted.[12]

But how did the performance of inflation targeters compare to the non-targeters? Every non-targeter had an average inflation rate below 3% in the last 10 years, giving credence to the argument that low inflation can be accomplished without an explicit inflation target. It should also be noted that inflation targeters did a better job of avoiding deflation (a fall in prices) than non-targeters. Among non-targeters in the past 10 years, Japan experienced 6 years of deflation, Singapore experienced 2 years, and Hong Kong experienced 5 years. By contrast, among targeters, only Israel and Luxembourg suffered from deflation (one year each). Both targeters and non-targeters enjoyed extremely stable inflation, as measured by the standard deviation of the inflation rate, with the exception of Israel and Hong Kong. Israel underwent a major disinflation (a decline in the inflation rate) around the time it adopted an inflation target, which would make the standard deviation large. Hong Kong's experience illustrates one of the drawbacks of a currency board: inflation is effectively determined by fluctuations in the demand for Hong Kong assets. When the demand for assets is volatile, the inflation rate will be volatile.

What about the critics' claim that inflation targeting would lead to excessively volatile economic growth? As measured by the output gap or the standard deviation of the growth rate (third and fourth column of Table 1), four economies (Australia, Canada, United Kingdom, Euro area) experienced more stable economic growth after the adoption of an inflation target, two economies were less stable (New Zealand and Israel), and two had mixed experiences (Sweden and Switzerland). This may suggest that, in practice, the political benefits of inflation targeting (e.g., preventing opportunistic behavior) may outweigh the economic disadvantages. It may also suggest that most targeters do not interpret their mandate literally. When faced with a choice between preventing an economic downturn or preventing inflation from rising slightly above its target, they choose the former and reduce interest rates, although a literal interpretation of their mandate would have them choose the latter and increase interest rates. In practice, inflation targeters seem to leave central banks more room for discretion and fine tuning than one might expect, and this does not appear to come at the expense of maintaining price stability.[13]

Compared to non-targeters, the economic growth of targeters is comparably stable. A few small countries were markedly more volatile than the rest, four of which were targeters (Iceland, Israel, New Zealand, and Sweden) and three non-targeters (Singapore, Hong Kong and Cyprus). Since smaller countries tend to be more vulnerable to external conditions beyond their control, one might expect their economies to be less stable. Among the rest of the countries, the results were broadly similar. Australia and Great Britain demonstrate that targeters can maintain economic stability for long periods of time, and the United States and Denmark demonstrate that non-targeters can do so as well. As for the concern that an inflation target would make a recession more serious, there does not seem to be any correlation between inflation targeting and countries with lower growth during the 2001-2002 economic slowdown. On average, Japan, a non-targeter, and the Euro Area and Switzerland, targeters, have experienced the lowest growth rates this decade. New Zealand, Australia, Canada, and the United Kingdom — all targeters — escaped the slowdown relatively unscathed. Nor is there strong evidence that negative output gaps were more likely to persist in countries with inflation targets. The United Kingdom and New Zealand had large and persistent output gaps throughout the early 1990s with an inflation target (while they were still in the transition phase of the target regime); on the other hand, Switzerland and Iceland in the early 1990s, and Japan in this decade, had similar difficulties without a target.

Bernanke et al. devise a series of tests to answer the question "How successful has inflation targeting been?" First, they ask "Does inflation targeting make disinflation less costly?" In other words, does the short run tradeoff between inflation and unemployment improve under an inflation targeting regime? To answer this question, they look at the predicted tradeoff based on data prior to the regime and compare it with the actual tradeoff after the regime. They do not find compelling evidence that inflation targeting improves the short-run tradeoff. Second, they ask "Does adoption of inflation targeting reduce inflationary expectations?" Based on survey and interest rate data, they find that inflationary expectations declined in all targeting countries after the adoption of the target, but not immediately. However, during that time inflationary expectations declined in non-targeting countries as well, suggesting there could be some other force driving expectations.[14] Finally, they ask "Does inflation targeting change the behavior of inflation?" For example, they hypothesize that if targeting improves central bank credibility and inflationary expectations, then there would be less pass-through from price shocks to long-term inflation. To answer this question, they forecast inflation rates based on data prior to the adoption of the targeting regime and compare it with actual rates achieved after the regime. They find that the actual rates are better than forecasted, suggesting targeting may improve the inflationary process in a benign way. However, actual rates were better than forecasted in many non-targeting countries as well. This suggests that more prudent central banking in general, rather than inflation targeting in particular, has changed the behavior of inflation.[15]

Now that the aggregate data have been analyzed, it may be useful to review the individual experiences of five key economies in greater depth to gain a richer understanding of how inflation targeting has worked out in practice.

New Zealand

Among the five economies highlighted in this article, New Zealand has the most detailed and structured program directing its central bank, the Reserve Bank of New Zealand, to follow a goal of price stability.[16]

New Zealand also has the longest experience with inflation targeting. On May 4, 1989, the government of New Zealand introduced the Reserve Bank of New Zealand Act. It was passed by parliament on December 15, 1989, and took effect on February 1, 1990. The act declared the "stability of the general level of prices shall be the overriding objective of monetary policy." No other subordinate objectives are mentioned in the act, although the administration of the act makes it possible for the Bank to focus on other goals such as GDP growth and employment.

Under the terms of the legislation, the Minister of Finance and the Reserve Bank Governor are required to make periodic *Policy Targets Agreements* (or PTAs) regarding the price index to be targeted and the allowable range of inflation that is consistent with the act. "Price stability" is defined in terms of an allowable but positive inflation rate rather than a stable *price level*, which would require any inflation that occurred to be offset by deflation.

The inflation goal is set by the government, and it is incumbent on the Reserve Bank to achieve it. The Governor of the Bank is required to report on the inflation performance twice per year and *may* be dismissed for failure to achieve the target at any time during his/her five-year term. Dismissal is not, however, automatic. As of this date, no Governor has been dismissed. To enhance the independence of the Bank, the government provided for its advanced funding for a five-year period (it should be noted that this advanced funding was specified in *nominal* terms, which should act as an added incentive to keep the inflation rate low). However, it would be wrong to view the Bank as anything other than an agency of the government. It does not have statutory independence even though it does have instrument independence in that it can vary interest rates to achieve its goal.

While the PTA fixed the consumer price index as the index for measuring inflation, it allowed the Reserve Bank to exclude from that measure of inflation the "first round" effects from changes in the international terms of trade, indirect taxes, natural disasters, disasters due to livestock disease outbreaks, and changes in the interest-cost component of the CPI. It is important to note that the Reserve Bank calculates the effect of these factors on the inflation rate. The calculations are not made by the government's statistical agency, Statistics New Zealand. Thus, the Reserve Bank prepares the inflation numbers against which it is evaluated. However, when these "escape clauses" are invoked, the Bank must formally communicate this to the government.

The core of this regime, as noted above, is the PTA. In the first one, dated March 1990, an eventual goal of holding inflation within a range of 0% to 2% was expressed. However, as an interim, the Reserve Bank announced that it would use as a "guidepost" a range for inflation at year's end of from 3% to 5%. It was emphasized that the target was intended to be a true range in that both floor and ceiling were important and that no special emphasis was to be placed on the midpoint. In actual practice, the inflation rate has frequently been near the upper bound of the range. The election that took place in December 1990 resulted in a new government. It worked out a new PTA with the Reserve Bank under which a new set of inflation goals were adopted for the period 1991-1993: 2.5% to 4.5% for the end of 1991, 1.5% to 3.5% for the end of 1992, and 0% to 2% for the end of 1993. Late in 1993, the government extended the 0% to 2% range for an indefinite period and specified that the inflation rate was to be contained within this range on a *continuous* basis. Since the consumer price index is only published quarterly, this means that the price stability goal must be met every quarter as opposed to being met on an average basis over the year or at the end of the year.[17]

The PTA negotiated in December 1996 had an indefinite time horizon and broadened the target range to 0% to 3%. Part of the reason for broadening the range was political. A newly emerging political party had campaigned on the basis that the prevailing range was too restrictive and that, as a result, it had an adverse effect on employment. In the election in 1996, this party came to hold the balance of power. After it joined the governing coalition, the range increase took place. A second reason for broadening the range was operational. The Reserve Bank complained that the narrow range and the need to meet the inflation target *continuously* caused undesirable instability in the instruments of monetary policy, meaning that often large fluctuations in interest rates and exchange rates took place. These fluctuations were thought to be disruptive to output growth and employment.

The PTA signed on September 17, 2002, involved several significant changes in the conduct of monetary policy. First, the targeted range was changed to 1% to 3% from 0% to 3%. Second, the target did not have to be achieved continuously. It was now to be met over the "medium term." Third, there appears to a subtle shift in emphasis in the sense that price stability now becomes more of a means to an end with the ultimate goal to "...promote sustainable and balanced economic development in order to create full employment, higher real income and a more equitable distribution of incomes." It is unclear at this time what this means in terms of compromising the price stability goal. It clearly diminishes accountability.

It should be emphasized that throughout the period in which monetary policy has been committed to a price stability goal, the Reserve Bank has continued to acknowledge that it still has a short-run objective of securing the financial stability of the country and to this end is prepared to act as a lender-of-last-resort. Such a necessity has not yet arisen, however. Moreover, the "escape clauses" allow the Bank to give some attention to such competing goals as GDP growth and unemployment. For example, should the Bank be forced to deflate the economy in the presence of an oil price hike (a "terms of trade" shock), it could have serious negative consequences for GDP growth and employment. By invoking the escape clause, the Bank can accommodate the shock and moderate its short run consequences for output and employment. On the downside, too many uses of the escape clause would render the inflation target meaningless.

The Reserve Bank has been aided in achieving its price stability goal by the efforts of the government to commit itself to a program of budget deficit reductions. Between 1986 and 1993, the budget was in deficit each year ranging between 0.7% and 4.6% of GDP.[18] From 1994 to 2004, the budget was in surplus each year. This move to budget surpluses has decreased the stress placed on the Reserve Bank to accommodate budget deficits, giving it greater independence to focus on achieving price stability.

An important element of this new regime was to establish the credibility of the price stability goal in the minds of economic agents. The reason for this is that expectations of inflation enter into a range of economic decision making, especially those related to wages, salaries, interest rates, and relative prices. When the expected inflation rate runs above the actual inflation rate, for example, wage settlements can be costly in terms of higher unemployment than would occur if this were not the case. Market interest rates can also be unduly high, implying high real interest rates which can discourage capital formation. Thus, an important element of New Zealand's new monetary regime is to promote transparency by providing information to the public about monetary policy, why decisions are made, how policy is executed to keep inflation within the targeted range, and what it seeks to accomplish (although, as noted above, there are still gaps in transparency.) Survey data indicate that inflationary expectations in New Zealand fell from double-digit rates in the 1980s until about 1992, and were stable through the rest of the period covered by the study.[19]

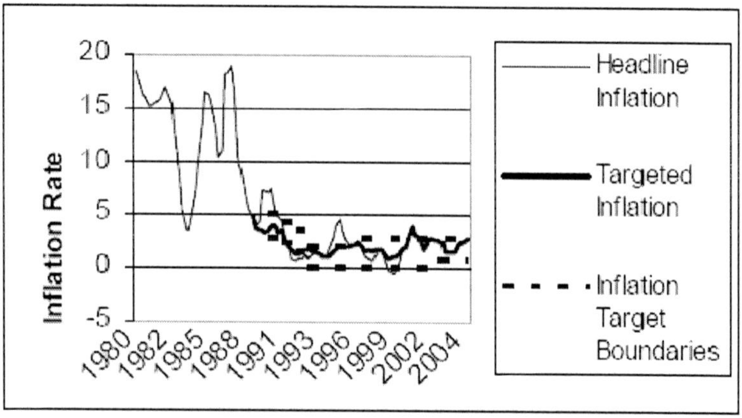

Source: Reserve Bank of New Zealand.

Notes: Inflation is measured as the 12-month change in the consumer price index. Targeted inflation is defined as underlying inflation until the September 1997 quarter, CPIX inflation (excluding interest and section prices) from the September 1999 quarter to the June 2000 quarter through to the June 1999 quarter, and CPI inflation from the September 1999 quarter to the present.

Figure 1. Inflation and Inflation Targeting in New Zealand

The evidence from Figure 1 suggests that the Reserve Bank has been able over most of this period to keep the underlying inflation rate within the targeted range. The bank has invoked the terms of trade escape clause three times, 1990-1991, 1994, and 2000-2001 to accommodate international oil price shocks. As noted above, giving the Bank discretion to invoke an escape clause does not come without a price: the transparency and credibility of policy is reduced. For example, the increase in oil prices in 1994 was not significant, yet the bank invoked an escape clause anyway. Without objective criteria determining when an escape clause can or cannot be invoked, it is possible for the escape clause to be used to deflect attention from demand-driven inflation that the Bank should have contained. Since market participants cannot replicate the Bank's decision-making process, an important part of this process becomes obscured. Market participants will always face uncertainty over the extent to which the Bank will adhere to its goal of keeping inflation within the 1% to 3% range. Explaining after the fact why it behaved as it did, does not necessarily aid transparency.

A case can be made that inflation targeting has yielded substantial benefits for New Zealand by comparing the period 1982-1989 with 1994-2001. As shown in Table 3, the average inflation rate under the new regime has fallen by more than 80%. This has been accompanied by a rise in the average unemployment rate. Averages may be deceptive, however. While it is true that between 1994 and 2001, unemployment averaged 6.6%, the rate has been falling and in 2001, it averaged 5.3%. (By 2004, it had fallen to 3.9%.) In the earlier period, it averaged 4.8%, but was on the rise, reaching 7.1% by 1990.[20] The average rate of growth of GDP over the years 1994-2001 was 3.1%. During the target period, GDP contracted in only one year, 1998, at the height of the Asian financial crisis. Thus, inflation targeting did not render New Zealand immune from this major regional economic shock. Over the period 1982-1989, GDP growth averaged 2.8%. This average was dominated by two years, 1984 (6.6%) and 1987 (6.8%); in five other years, it was under 2%, and during 1983, GDP grew only 0.1%. Another way to measure economic performance is to see how close actual GDP is to potential or full-employment GDP. Over the period 1994-2001, the absolute average of the output gap was 1.0%. During the 1982-1989 period, it was 1.9%, or nearly twice as large. During both 2000 and 2001, New Zealand's GDP was very near to its potential.[21]

The transition period in which the new regime was being implemented, 1990-1993, was not without cost. The inflation rate declined from 6.2% in 1990 to 1.7% in 1993. GDP growth was flat in 1990, -1.7% in 1991, and 0.7% in 1992. In 1993, it resumed at a healthy 5.2%. Reflecting the performance of actual GDP, the output gap deteriorated from 0.6% in 1990 to -3.5% in 1992. The unemployment rate rose from 7.8% in 1990 to a high of 10.3% in 1991 and 1992.

To gauge how the Bank has balanced its price stability mandate with the desire for economic stability in practice, it is useful to look more closely at two episodes where the regime arguably was tested (1997-1998, 2000). In 1997-1998, the Bank had to react to contagion effects from the Asian Crisis, characterized by a fall in exports to leading trading partners, an exchange rate appreciation with affected Asian countries that put pressure on import-competing industries, and worldwide financial unrest. The Bank held short-term interest rates steady in 1997 and the first half of 1998, despite the fact that inflation was falling and well within the target range in the second half of 1997. The economy began to contract in 1998. The Bank then lowered rates significantly in the second half of 1998. Perhaps the Bank would have reacted more strongly to the negative shock had it not been for its sole goal mandate. On the other hand, the effects of the crisis may have been more serious than the Bank anticipated. Looking at the Bank's *Monetary Policy Statements* from the time, it appears that the Bank initially underestimated the negative effect the crisis would have on GDP and overestimated the positive effect it would have on inflation (because the trade-weighted exchange rate was depreciating).

Table 3. Economic Indicators in New Zealand (Data in percentages)

	1982-1989 (avg.)	**1994-2001 (avg.)**	**2004**
Inflation Rate	10.8	2.0	2.3
GDP Growth Rate	2.8	3.1	5.0
Unemployment Rate	4.8	6.6	3.9
Output Gap (% of GDP)	1.9	1.0	2.4
Fiscal Balance (% of GDP)	-3.1	1.7	3.5

Source: All data except unemployment are from the International Monetary Fund; unemployment data are from OECD.

Note: Average output gap is the average of the absolute value. Inflation rate is measured by the consumer price index.

In late 2000, the inflation rate unexpectedly rose a full percentage point above the target, despite a monetary tightening that began earlier in the year. The rise in oil prices that year probably contributed to this rise in inflation. Interestingly, the Bank did not tighten policy further when inflation moved above the target, citing the transitory nature of the oil shock. In fact, the Bank undertook a slight easing in policy in mid-2001, despite the fact that inflation was still slightly above the 3% target boundary. This easing was presumably in response to the contraction of GDP in the first quarter of 2001. Thus, faced with a clear choice between an inflation rate that was above target and a slowing economy, the Bank did not take sharp measures to rein in inflation as the "sole goal" mandate suggests to some. The target may have made the Bank's response to the slowdown more moderate than it otherwise would have been, however.

Canada

The Bank of Canada's commitment to a goal of price stability was not the result of legislation amending the Bank Act to make price stability the exclusive focus of monetary policy. Rather, the effort to commit the Bank to this goal began in 1988 as a personal campaign by the then Bank Governor, John Crow. His efforts culminated in the joint announcement by the Minister of Finance and the Governor of the Bank on February 26, 1991 of formal targets for "reducing inflation and establishing price stability in Canada."[22] (The announcement date was carefully chosen to attract public attention as it was the day on which the government announced its budget.) This was, then, a policy of the government and the Bank. It was not a change in the Bank of Canada Act. Such a cooperative or joint effort continues to this day with the inflation target being jointly determined and announced by the government and the Bank.[23]

As in New Zealand, price stability was defined in terms of a targeted rate of inflation rather than a stable price level. However, a precise definition was not given initially to the term "price stability" since the government and the Bank were uncertain about how the economy would behave in an environment of price stability. However, at the outset, the Bank stated that "price stability" meant an inflation rate below 2%.

The joint announcement specified that it was desired that the rate of inflation would fall between 2% and 4% by the end of 1992 (some 22 months beyond the date of the announcement), to between 1.5% and 3.5% by mid-1994, and to between 1% and 3% by the end of 1995. The 1% to 3% range has been continuously reconfirmed to the present day.[24] Setting out the path to price stability in the initial announcement was thought to be important in building expectations of economic agents and the credibility of the Bank in achieving such a goal. Studying the inflationary expectations of the public over this time can determine how successful the target has been in this regard. One study found evidence that inflation targeting lowered the inflationary expectations of the public quickly, from over 5% shortly before the target was introduced to 2% in 1996.[25] But another study found that inflation targeting had no rapid effect on inflationary expectations, and, to the extent that expectations fell, they remained above the target range.[26]

Several aspects of the joint announcement should be noted. First, the initial target range was to apply nearly two years after the announcement. This was done on the grounds that monetary changes taken today would have their effects in the future (or in the words of economists, the lag involved between the initial change in monetary policy and its ultimate effect on the economy can be both long and of a variable length). It was also done to increase the likelihood of success since substantial progress in achieving the goal would have been made. Second, the targets did not have to be met continuously over any given period. They were to be achieved by some specific date. Third, the initial announcement made it sound as though the objective to be targeted was the midpoint of the range. This has not been the practice, however, as the Bank has not moved aggressively to force the rate to the midpoint of the range when it has lingered at or below the lower bound of the range. Fourth, "price stability" in the Canadian context originally meant an inflation rate that was below 2.0%, the mid-point of the 1% to 3% range that was to be achieved by the end of 1995. How much below was not specified. In December 1993, a decision was made to continue the 1% to 3% range until the end of 1998. Subsequent decisions have extended this range to the present.

Although the targeted inflation rate range is specified in terms of the total consumer price index, the Bank of Canada, in practice, conducts monetary policy based on a modified CPI because it is interested in the trend rate of inflation, and the actual course taken by the CPI can be influenced temporarily by the prices of such volatile items as food and energy and more permanently by such one-time events as changes in indirect taxes. Thus, the Bank uses a modified CPI that excludes the eight most volatile components of the CPI. This index is computed by Statistics Canada rather than by the Bank itself. Thus, unlike the Reserve Bank of New Zealand, the Bank of Canada does not compute the index against which it is evaluated. For example, in 1994 headline inflation briefly fell below 0%. But the Bank interpreted the effect to be caused by a reduction in sales tax rates, and did not change the stance of monetary policy.

While supply side deviations of the inflation rate from the targeted range are likely to be tolerated, demand side deviations are not. In this respect, the 1% to 3% range can lead to a countercyclical monetary policy in the sense that an inflation rate above 3%, a sign of excess demand, leads to monetary tightening while an inflation rate below 1% is taken as symptomatic of weak demand, prompting an easing of monetary policy. In this sense, targeting inflation is held to be compatible with goals of high employment and maximum income growth.

Accountability in the Canadian framework is weaker than that of New Zealand. The Minister of Finance cannot fire the Governor of the Bank for a failure to achieve the inflation goal. The Minister can issue a "policy directive" ordering a change in policy such as moving the interest rate in a given direction. This possibility, however, must add some uncertainty to the perception of economic agents about the independence of the Bank to pursue the price stability goal. No such directive has yet been issued, and some analysts argue that the policy directive does not pose a credible threat to central bank independence because the government is unlikely to ever issue a directive. As in New Zealand, the Bank of Canada has made a large effort toward greater policy transparency by communicating to the public its assessment of the economy, the role played by monetary policy in the behavior of the economy, and the rationale for its decisions. Since 1995, the Bank of Canada has issued a semi-annual *Monetary Policy Report*.

The government and the Bank recognize that under certain circumstances the inflation targets can be breached. These are not enumerated at great length as in New Zealand, but clearly large increases in oil prices or a widespread natural disaster would be examples that might require appropriate action by the Bank even though it could threaten the Bank's commitment to price stability. Whether to accommodate these shocks was left to the discretion of the Bank. In some circumstances in which the inflation rate was pushed above the upper bound of the targeted range, the Bank would be expected to return the rate to the midpoint of the range, but not below it. From the data it would appear that the Bank of Canada has managed to cope with oil price shocks and the major changes in the relationship of the Canadian to the U.S. dollar. (Between March 1991 and November 2002, the Canadian dollar fell from U.S.$0.86 to $0.64, a depreciation in nominal terms of about 26%.) The data in Figure 2 show that the Bank of Canada has had a good deal of success meeting its price stability target.

In support of the price stability goal, the government of Canada adopted official targets for the reduction of the federal budget deficit — the Spending Control Act of 1992. Significant budget deficit reductions have been achieved and, as in New Zealand, this has reduced pressure on the Bank of Canada to accommodate the government, thus strengthening the ability of the Bank to focus monetary policy on achieving price stability.[27] Between 1990 and 1995, the budget deficit of the federal government fluctuated between 5.3% and 9.1% of GDP. In 1996, the deficit declined to 2.8% of GDP and from 1997 through 2004, the budget was in surplus ranging from 0.2% to 2.9% of GDP.

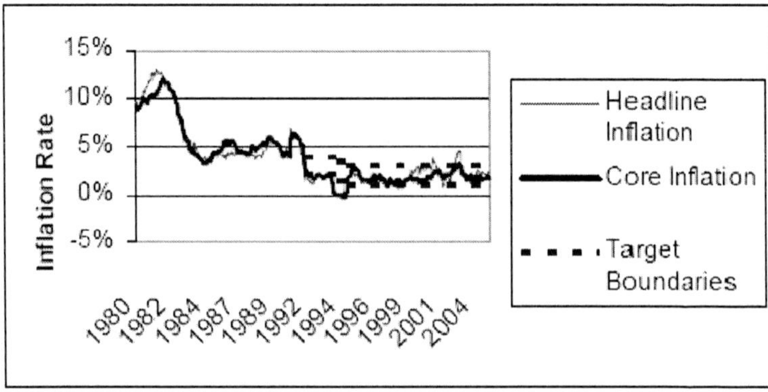

Source: Bank of Canada; Federal Reserve Bank of Kansas City; Haver Analytics.

Notes: Inflation is measured as the 12-month change in the consumer price index. Until May 2001, core inflation is defined as headline inflation excluding food and energy. After May 2001, core inflation is defined as headline inflation excluding the eight most volatile components.

Figure 2. Inflation and Inflation Targeting in Canada

The performance of the Canadian economy since the price stability regime was fully implemented has been impressive, as shown in Table 4. The average inflation rate under the target was nearly 50% lower than in the years before the target. Between 1996 and 2001, real GDP grew at an average rate of 3.6% and was positive each year. Moreover, Canada managed to avoid the contraction in GDP experienced by the U.S. in 2001, an unexpected result since nearly 40% of Canadian GDP is exported to the United States. Over the period 1986-1991, before the target was adopted, GDP growth was positive in five of the six years and averaged 2.1%.[28] The absolute average of the output gap during 1996-2001 was 0.9%. During 1986-1992, the gap averaged 1.6%, nearly twice as high. The unemployment rate averaged nearly the same over both periods, 8.9% vs. 8.7%. Averages do not tell the whole story, however. During 1996-2001, the rate fell from 9.6% to 7.2% while during the earlier period, the rate rose from a low 7.5% to a high of 10.3%. The transition period to the new regime, 1992-1995, was not an easy one. The inflation rate was 4.8% in 1992 and 5.2% in 1993. It fell to 1.5% in 1994. GDP registered very slow growth in 1992 and 1994, and contracted 2.1% in 1993. Unemployment was above 11% in 1992 and 1993.[29]

Table 4. Economic Indicators in Canada (data in percentages)

	1986-1991 (avg.)	1996-2001 (avg.)	2004
Inflation Rate	4.7	2.5	1.8
GDP Growth Rate	2.1	3.6	2.8
Unemployment Rate	8.7	8.9	7.2
Output Gap (% of GDP)	1.6	0.9	-0.1
Fiscal Balance (% of GDP)	-5.9	0.7	1.4

Source: All data except unemployment are from the International Monetary Fund; unemployment data are from OECD.

Note: Average output gap is the average of the absolute value. Inflation rate is measured by the consumer price index.

United Kingdom

In October 1992, the Chancellor of the Exchequer announced that the focus of British monetary policy was to be shifted to controlling inflation.[30] This followed Britain's withdrawal from the European Exchange Rate Mechanism whose system of fixed exchange rates had served as an anchor for British monetary policy.[31]

The fact that the announcement was made by the Chancellor is significant in that the then-subordinate position of the Bank of England to the government was continued (the Chancellor, rather than the Bank Governor, set monetary policy). Neither its autonomy nor independence was enhanced by the change in focus. In fact, this was simply a policy change by the government and involved no change in the statutes governing the Bank. Thus, the new policy could be reversed at any time.[32]

According to the Chancellor's announcement, the goal was to hold the inflation rate, as measured by the retail price index less the mortgage interest component, to a range of 1% to 4% per year with an expectation that the rate would be below 2.5% by the end of the then sitting parliament (which would be no later than the spring of 1997).[33] (In December 2003, the targeted inflation rate was switched to the consumer price index (CPI)). Thus, the index used to measure inflation included both food and energy. This meant that the British chose to include such things as oil price shocks in their target. Moreover, there was no list of special exceptions to meeting the targets for shocks such as in the New Zealand legislation. As the prevailing inflation rate at the time of the announcement was below 4%, a goal of keeping it below 4% was thought to be not very ambitious. The range of the inflation target set by the Chancellor was originally intended to limit the scope for both slippage and counter-cyclical policy. Later, the width of the range was interpreted as representing the view that monetary policy could only *imperfectly control* the inflation rate. In June 1995, the range of 1% to 4% was replaced by a point target of 2.5% that was to be met on a continuous basis. Since the point target was not (and could not be) continuously met, it implied that some deviations were to be tolerated.

In this initial step to change the monetary regime, the Chancellor set the inflation target. The Bank of England provided a two-year inflation forecast on a quarterly basis (based on such factors as the level of unemployment, GDP growth, the fiscal position of the government, and the growth rate of various measures of money), together with a recommendation on the base interest rate, its major tool for implementing monetary policy. The Chancellor decided whether or not to follow the Bank's recommendation. Thus, in this arrangement, the policy target was not the current inflation rate, but rather the rate expected to prevail two years in the future. It was upon this forecast that the Bank made its recommendation on the current position to take by monetary policy.[34] Several times during these early years, the Chancellor overruled the recommendations of the Bank to change the base rate.

A problem with this arrangement, that was perceived early on, was that since the Chancellor controlled the base interest rate, the policy variable, a refusal to raise or lower it following recommendations of the Bank of England, could be interpreted in a variety of ways (e.g., that the Chancellor disagreed with the Bank's inflation forecast, or that there was a difference in their respective commitments to the inflation goal). This arguably tended to obscure transparency and weaken accountability and probably also worked to raise expectations of inflation.

Subsequently, steps were taken by the government that both increased the independence of the Bank of England and provided greater information about monetary policy. Beginning in February 1993, the Bank began to issue a quarterly *Inflation Report* presenting the Bank's assessment of inflation prospects and the views of the staff and officers about economic matters in general. The then Chancellor promised not to edit these reports but allow them to become public as written by the Bank. Subsequent to September 1992, the Chancellor and the Governor instituted formal consultative meetings designed to formulate the implementation of monetary policy (i.e., changing interest rates to achieve the inflation goal). In April 1994, the Chancellor agreed to the publication of the minutes of these monthly meetings after a lapse of six weeks (this replaced a lapse of 30 years). There was no doubt, however, that it was the Chancellor who made the ultimate decision about interest rate changes even though the Bank was given control over the precise timing of the changes. This makes the United Kingdom a unique case in that it may have been the only country to adopt an inflation target without giving its central bank instrument independence (i.e., control over interest rates). Since both inflation targeting and central bank independence are the two major institutional changes that have been credited with generating the worldwide decline in inflation in the 1990s, it is interesting to note that Britain achieved price stability with the former but not the latter.

This situation changed on May 6, 1997. The incoming Labour government announced that from then on the Bank of England would be given control over changes in the base interest rates that it felt were necessary to achieve the government's inflation target. Decisions on moving the base interest rate were to be made by a newly created nine-member Monetary Policy Committee. Five of the nine members are Bank of England officers, including the Governor and Deputy Governor. The remaining four are appointed by the government. All serve for a term of three years and are eligible for reappointment. The elected government, however, retained a "national interest" control over monetary policy which allows it to override the decisions of the Committee on moving the base interest rate in pursuit of the inflation guidelines. No overrides have yet occurred and the law is silent on the conditions under which such an override can be invoked. Thus, the Bank was given instrument independence, but not goal independence. On June 12, 1997, just prior to the first meeting of the Monetary Policy Committee, the Chancellor announced that the inflation target would remain 2.5%, but should the actual rate deviate from the target by more than one percentage point (in either direction), it was to trigger a report from the Committee explaining why this had happened, what policy actions were to be taken to deal with it, and when the inflation rate was expected to be back on target. In December 2003, the target was changed to 2%, as measured by the CPI.

Possibly, there are two weaknesses in the current regime. First, the inflation target is set by the government, and the Bank of England is expected to achieve this target subject to an override by the government if required in the "national interest." This ambiguity, it can be argued, makes it difficult for economic agents to discern a clear signal of the seriousness of the government's commitment to achieve its goal. Second, a government can only set an inflation target that lasts while it has a majority in the parliament. When a parliament comes to an end, a question can arise whether inflation in excess of the target will be remediated or whether bygones will be bygones. This, and the possibility of a new target, can also cause uncertainty for economic agents. This may be an inherent limitation of targeting, for no democratic government is likely to surrender its right to determine economic policy to an unelected body. However, as noted above, adherence to a target, once set, seems to be a litmus test for monetary responsibility.

Although the United Kingdom achieved price stability before the Bank's independence was enhanced, there is evidence that independence had a significant effect on inflationary expectations. A measure of inflationary expectations derived from bond yields suggests that it had trended downward after the implementation of the inflation target in 1992. The sharpest drop in expectations came after the Bank of England was made operationally independent in 1997. Since then inflationary expectations have dropped from over 4% to about 2.5%, equal to the inflation target.[35]

The new monetary regime did not initially enjoy a supporting fiscal policy. The initial announcement of the shift in monetary policy did not coincide with any statutory commitment to bring down the then-large budget deficit that in 1992 was 6.4% of GDP. It rose to a high of 7.9% of GDP in 1993. It then began a decline, and by 1998 a surplus of 0.4% of GDP was recorded. While the average fiscal deficit in both periods was virtually the same, as shown in Table 5, the two periods are really quite different. The deficit trended upward during the 1984-1992 period, with only one year of surplus (1988), while it trended downward from 1993 to 2001, with surpluses from 1998 to 2001. Since 2002, the budget has returned to deficit.

Table 5. Economic Indicators in United Kingdom (Data in percentages)

	1984-1992 (avg.)	1993-2001 (avg.)	2004
Inflation Rate	5.3	2.6	1.3
GDP Growth Rate	2.4	3.0	3.1
Unemployment Rate	9.0	7.2	4.8
Output Gap (% of GDP)	1.2	0.9	0.4
Fiscal Balance (% of GDP)	-2.3	-2.2	-3.0

Source: All data except unemployment are from the International Monetary Fund; unemployment data are from OECD.

Notes: Average output gap is the average of the absolute value. Inflation rate is measured by the retail price index.

In spite of perceived institutional shortcomings, the new emphasis of price stability has yielded impressive results. Since the adoption of the regime, the inflation rate shown in Figure 3 has been kept very close to

2.5%, which was markedly lower than during the previous 10 years. The British have had no difficulty achieving price stability in spite of the inclusion of food and energy in their targeted price index. Quite clearly, the U.K. has now had more than a decade of low inflation, in marked contrast with the wide fluctuations during the preceding decade. The data in Table 5 show that the average inflation rate has been cut by half and this has not had an adverse consequence on the major performance indicators of the British economy. GDP has registered positive growth in each year from 1993 through 2004 and has averaged nearly 3% per year.[36] From 1984 to 1992, GDP contracted in one year (1991) and recorded no growth in another (1992) and averaged 2.4%. Like New Zealand and Canada, a major disinflation accompanied this contraction, with inflation falling from 8.1% in 1990 to 3% in 1993. However, most of the disinflation occurred before the new targeting regime was even announced. The unemployment rate in the U.K. has fallen from 9.4% in 1993 to 5.1% in 2001. Over this period, it averaged 7.2%. (In 2004, it fell to 4.8%.) From 1984-1992, unemployment averaged 9% and was below 6% in only one year. The absolute average of the output gap from 1993 through 2001 was 0.9% compared with 1.2% over 1984-1992. Over both periods, it was very large in only one year, 1993 (-2.3%).

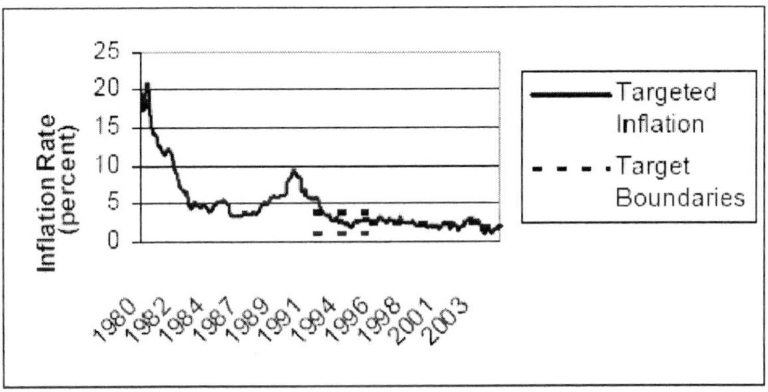

Source: Bank of England.

Notes: Targeted inflation is measured as the 12-month change in the retail price index excluding mortgage interest payments until December 2003. From December 2003 on, it is measured as the consumer price index.

Figure 3. Inflation and Inflation Targeting in the United Kingdom

Sweden

On January 15, 1993, two months after Sweden had abandoned a fixed exchange rate that had anchored its monetary system for many years, the governing board of the Swedish Riksbank (the central bank) decided that a price stability goal could serve as a viable alternative anchor. This shift in regime was not planned, but forced on the Riksbank. It announced as a goal that price stability was to be achieved at the end of 1995. The Board defined price stability as a 2% inflation rate as measured by the consumer price index with a tolerance band of plus and minus 1%. The announcement made no mention of the possible path to be taken by prices during the two-year transition period. The length of the transition period was justified on two grounds. First, the Riksbank did not have much experience operating in a flexible exchange rate regime and, second, monetary policy operates with a long lag.[37]

While the goal was set in terms of an inflation rate as measured by the full CPI, in subsequent reports the Riksbank has made reference to different measures of an underlying rate of inflation as given by the CPI less various components such as food, energy, and changes in indirect taxes and subsidies. These other measures are offered as evidence of the inflationary pressures faced by the country. Moreover, while it was initially understood that there were to be no exceptions to the price stability goal, subsequent statements from the Riksbank indicate that this is not the case. The goal may be relaxed in the face of major changes in taxes and subsidies and unforeseen external shocks.

Initially, it was unclear whether the target was to be met continuously or only over a given time period. This uncertainty was ultimately cleared up with the Riksbank specifying that the target was to be met over the most recent four quarters. Breaches of the target band trigger a report from the Bank, at least annually, explaining why this occurred. It does not require remediation — bygones are, apparently, bygones. Curiously, while the target is specified in terms of the full CPI, when inflation measured by this index fell below the 1% lower bound of the target range during 1996-1997 and 1999-2000 (see Figure 4), the Bank did not take action to bring the rate back within the targeted range. Rather, it spoke of transitory factors as the cause of the lower inflation rate and stressed that its measure of the core inflation rate was generally within the targeted range. This appeared to indicate that the Bank has shifted to the core rate as the target *de facto*. This raises questions about the transparency and accountability that the target is meant to promote.

In summary, the new regime for monetary policy and the target for price stability was instituted and set by the Riksbank itself. It was not legislated by the Swedish parliament, even though the government later endorsed the goal. This should not be taken to mean that the Riksbank is independent of the government. It is not. Four of the seven members of the Governing Board, including the Chairman, are appointed by the governing party (or parties); three are appointed by the opposition party (or parties). Historically, these appointees have been members of parliament. Nevertheless, adopting a price stability goal has increased the operational independence of the Board to implement policy. Since the new policy goal was announced by the Riksbank and not the government, it did not contain anything in the way of accountability for a failure to achieve the goal. This is, perhaps, an important weakness in the new Swedish monetary regime. Moreover, the Bank has never issued a document outlining the operating details of the new regime. This lack of transparency is at odds with the practices of the three other countries surveyed in this study. Nevertheless, if inflationary expectations are any guide, the new regime has been viewed by the public as credible. Between 1994 and 1997, inflationary expectations fell from above 4% to about 2%.[38]

It can be seen from Figure 4 that the Riksbank has managed to keep the inflation rate markedly lower than in the previous 15 years. However, the headline inflation rate has been below the lower bound of the targeted range nearly as frequently as it has been within the range, at times falling below zero. This suggests to some observers that monetary policy may be a good deal tighter in Sweden than policymakers are willing to concede. The Bank's position is that the low inflation rate is due to "transitory" factors to which it is unwilling to respond. The behavior of the unemployment rate provides support to both sides. The Bank can point to the sharp reduction in the unemployment rate during the new regime. The Swedish unemployment rate was at or close to 8.0% during 1993-1997. By 2001, it had been halved to 4.0%; since then, it increased to 5.5% in 2004. However, critics point out that between 1987 and 1992, a comparable period prior to the new regime, the unemployment rate varied between 1.5% and 5.0%. As shown in Table 6, the average unemployment rate during the new regime is more than twice as high as during 1987-1992.

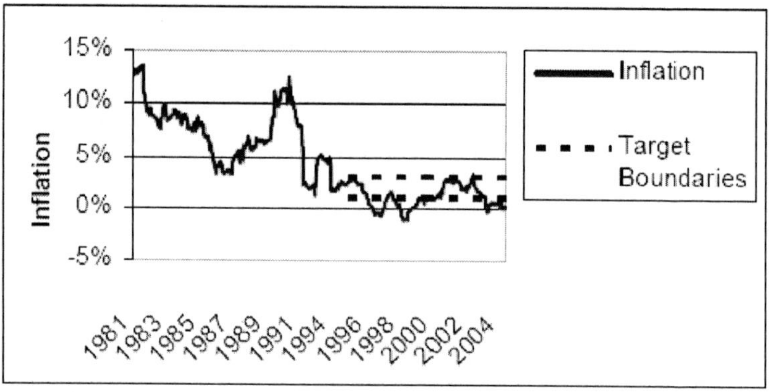

Source: Riksbank; Federal Reserve Bank of Kansas City.

Notes: Inflation is measured as the 12-month change in the consumer price index. Core inflation excludes the effects of indirect taxes and subsidies.

Figure 4. Inflation and Inflation Targeting in Sweden

Table 6. Economic Indicators in Sweden (data in percentages)

	1987-1992 (avg.)	1996-2001 (avg.)	2004
Inflation Rate	6.4	0.8	1.1
GDP Growth Rate	1.3	2.7	3.5
Unemployment Rate	2.6	6.1	5.5
Output Gap (% of GDP)	3.2	2.1	-0.1
Fiscal Balance (% of GDP)	1.4	1.3	0.7

Source: All data except unemployment are from the International Monetary Fund; unemployment data are from OECD.

Notes: Average output gap is the average of the absolute value. Inflation rate is measured by the consumer price index.

Other performance characteristics suggest that inflation targeting has been successful. In the first six years the targeting regime was fully implemented, 1996-2001, GDP growth was positive each year and averaged 2.7% per year. During the six years prior to the transition to the targeting regime, 1987-1992, GDP grew by 1.3% on average.[39] It contracted for three years in the early 1990s (1991, 1992, and 1993). The absolute average of the output gap was 2.1% during the new regime, compared to 3.2% over 1987-1992. This suggests growth was more stable under the targeting regime. However, the gap was very large and negative from 1996-1998. During the transition period, 1993-1995, inflation fell from 4.6% to 2.5%. GDP growth, negative in 1993, showed a strong rebound in both 1994

(4.1%) and 1995 (3.7%). The output gap fell from -5.8% to -2.8%, while the unemployment rate declined from 8.2% to 7.7%.

When the Riksbank announced the new monetary regime in 1993, the Swedish fiscal position was one of a large budget deficit. The actual deficit, reflecting Sweden's serious economic downturn, was nearly 12% of GDP. Indeed, one of the objectives of targeting the inflation rate was to reassure economic agents that the Bank was not going to monetize the deficits. While the fiscal position of the government in the two periods appears to be the same, the average masks important differences. Between 1987 and 1992, the budget had shifted from a surplus of 4.1% of GDP to a deficit of 7.5%. Between 1996 and 2001, the budget had moved from a deficit of 3.4% of GDP to a surplus of 4.8%. The budget has been in surplus since 1998, and stood at 0.7% of GDP in 2004. This shift in the fiscal position of the government has been noted in various issues of the Bank's quarterly *Inflation Report* and is an important variable influencing the conduct of monetary policy.[40] Thus, the goal of price stability received support from fiscal policy.

Recent events offer a good illustration of how the Riksbank interprets its price stability mandate. When core inflation rose slightly above the target boundary in late 2001, the economy was experiencing an economic slowdown. When faced with the conflict between maintaining price stability and combating the slowdown, the Riksbank initially lowered interest rates modestly. When inflation remained above the upper bound of the target range in early 2002, the Riksbank reversed the earlier interest rate cut. Inflation fell back within the target range shortly afterward, and was soon after near the lower bound of the target.

The Euro Area

The euro area's adoption of the goal of price stability is unique in the world: it is the only instance in which the goal was adopted at the currency's founding.[41] Then again, the euro is a unique political development in itself. On January 1, 1999, the European Central Bank took over responsibility for monetary policy in the countries of the euro area. As of 2002, 12 countries have willingly given up their currency and control of their monetary policy, and handed it to a newly created multi-country institution, the European Central Bank (ECB), which has a high degree of political independence and is directly answerable only to the European Union (EU). Furthermore, to ensure the Euro's success, the countries of the EU have placed significant limitations on their fiscal policy and public debt, as discussed below.

The sole goal of price stability is enshrined in the multi-national treaty between sovereign governments of the EU that brought the euro and ECB into existence. This makes it much more difficult to change than the mandate of most central banks, since it can only be changed if the treaty is amended. The specific numerical inflation target was not specified in the treaty, however. It was independently chosen by the ECB's Governing Council to support the price stability goal, and can be changed at any time at the ECB's discretion. Interestingly, the definition they chose was inflation of less than 2%, not explicitly specifying whether this represented a band from 0-2% and if there was a preferred midpoint to the band. One should note that the 2% target has precedence in the EU and was not chosen arbitrarily: in the years leading up to the euro, the council of the EU instructed all prospective members of the euro to bring their inflation rate down to 2%. This is somewhat analogous to the transition period that many countries adopt when implementing an inflation target in which inflation is allowed to slowly decline down to the targeted rate.

Many of the other details surrounding the target were not included in the treaty either. The Governing Council decided that the inflation target should be achieved over the medium term, and that inflation would be defined by the 12 month change in the harmonized index of consumer prices (HICP) for the euro area as a whole (policy will not be directed towards unique inflationary developments in individual countries). The ECB decided against targeting a core inflation rate or identifying "escape clauses" when the target would not have to be met.

Credibility is always an important issue for central bankers and one of the main arguments used by inflation target proponents. The ECB faced a unique credibility problem: it has no past record on which to stake its reputation. For political reasons, many participants felt that the ECB could achieve credibility if it could establish continuity with the Bundesbank, the German central bank which was known for its tough anti-inflationary stance. This was one reason that the sole goal of price stability was enshrined in the founding treaty. It also helps explain why the growth rate of the monetary aggregates is given a prominent role in the ECB's decision making, despite the fact that targeting the aggregates will sometimes contradict the inflation target: restraining the growth of the monetary aggregates had traditionally played a prominent role in Bundesbank policy.

Accountability and transparency are provided through annual and quarterly reports to the European Parliament, publication of the ECB's inflation forecast, and press releases immediately following the monthly meetings of the ECB Governing Council, which determine changes in monetary policy. There are no formal penalties in place if the inflation target is missed, however, and the meeting minutes and voting records of individual members of the Governing Council are not released.

As is the case with individual countries, large budget deficits can make the goal of price stability more difficult for the ECB to achieve. Indeed, a shared monetary policy creates greater incentives for individual countries to run large budget deficits than would normally occur when the fiscal and monetary authorities represent the same government. That is, individual countries could benefit by increasing their budget deficits to the detriment of the other members of the euro area since budget deficits would tend to push interest rates up across the euro area. Individual countries may also be less concerned about debt default if they think the ECB would be willing to bail them out.

To offset the debt incentive problem, the EU adopted the "Stability and Growth Pact," which limits euro members to budget deficits under 3% of GDP, unless the member's economy shrank by at least 0.75%, and limits member sovereign debt to less than 60% of GDP. Since a number of countries wishing to join the euro already had debt levels above 60% of GDP, this requirement was modified to require members to adopt a future debt path that would lead them to a debt level of 60% of GDP. To enforce the pact, the EU had the right to fine offending countries up to 0.5% of their GDP. These fiscal strictures are undoubtedly harsher than those that most other sovereign countries face: U.S. budget deficits were higher than 3% of GDP for most of the period from 1982-1993, and again since 2003. However, if the countries in the euro area are compared to, say, the state governments in the United States operating in the "dollar area," then the strictures do not appear particularly harsh at all. Nearly all American states are legally required to run balanced budgets and cannot be bailed out by the Federal Reserve if they default (although they could theoretically be bailed out by the federal government).[42]

In the first three years of the euro, all euro area countries met the requirements of the Stability and Growth Pact and budget deficits were significantly smaller than in preceding years (see Table 7). However, several of the countries ran a small budget deficit despite experiencing relatively robust economic growth. Unfortunately, budget deficits grow when economic growth falls, due to declines in tax revenues and automatic increases in expenditures. When the euro area's economy slowed in 2002, it became clear that several countries were unlikely to fulfill the pact's requirements. To date, no fines were assessed for these violations although the offending countries took no remedial action, and at this time the pact's future is in question as a result.

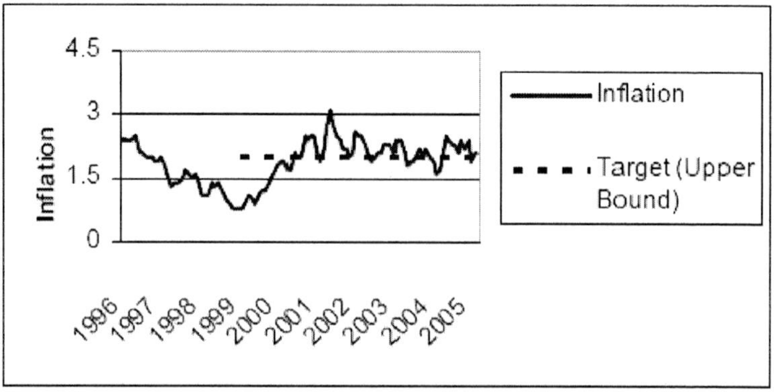

Source: European Central Bank

Note: Inflation is measured as the 12-month change in the Harmonized Index of Consumer Prices.

Figure 5. Inflation and Inflation Targeting in the Euro Area

As seen in, the ECB has successfully kept the inflation rate low, but not as low as its target. From June 2000 to 2005, the HPIC was at or slightly above the upper bound of 2% in most months. This occurred despite the fact that economic growth was weak from 2001 to 2004, as seen in Table 7. Growth was relatively robust in 1999 and 2000, but over the last decade it has fallen short of the growth rates enjoyed by the United States. The overall growth rate in the 2000s masks the fact that the countries on the "periphery" such as Ireland and Greece have enjoyed rapid rates of growth, while countries at the "core" such as Italy and Germany have lagged behind. High unemployment has been a problem for the euro area since the 1980s, and the inflation target made little difference in that regard, as expected. Average unemployment was a little lower than the previous decade in the 2000s. Research suggests that inflation targeting has had little effect so far on inflationary expectations in the three-year old euro area. While inflationary expectations reached their lowest point in 15 years in 2000, they reached their highest point — well above the target's upper bound — since 1993 in late 2001.[43]

Table 7. Economic Indicators in Euro Area

	1989-1998 (avg.)	1999-2003 (avg.)	2004
Inflation Rate	3.0	2.0	2.2
GDP Growth Rate	2.2	1.9	2.0
Unemployment Rate	12.7	8.4	8.4
Output Gap (% of GDP)	1.7	0.9	-1.6
Fiscal Balance (% of GDP)	-4.5	-1.9	-2.6

Source: All data except unemployment are from the International Monetary Fund; unemployment data are from OECD.

Notes: Average output gap (1989-1998) is the average of the absolute value. Inflation rate is measured by the HPIC.

In its first few years of policymaking, the ECB has come under significant criticism.[44] Critics charge that the Bank has been too slow to respond to changing economic conditions. These critics have become particularly vocal since economic growth in the euro area began to slow in 2001. Growth has been below 2% since 2001. In some countries, such as Germany and Italy, growth has been lower than the average. The critics claim that the ECB should have cut interest rates more aggressively, as the Fed did, to counter the downturn. From October 2000 to June 2003, the ECB cut the overnight interest rate from 4.75% to 2%. During that time, the Federal Reserve lowered overnight interest rates by 5.5 percentage points to 1%. Critics have also claimed that the Bank has not been sufficiently transparent, pointing to the fact that financial markets have expected a more expansionary policy than the Bank has delivered.

The irony of this criticism is that the Bank appears to be doing exactly what one would expect from a central bank whose sole goal is price stability. From June 2000 to 2005, the HPIC was typically at or above the upper bound of 2%. While the economic slowdown would be expected to quell inflationary pressures, it did not do so enough to offset other developments that were boosting prices, such as the oil price spike. It is difficult to see how the Bank could have cut interest rates more aggressively without ignoring its target. And since it never deviated from its target, its actions should have been transparent. In this light, the misperception on the part of financial markets seems to be due to their belief that the Bank would pursue its mandate less aggressively than it did.

The Experience of Developing Countries that Focus Monetary Policy on a Goal of Price Stability

Central banks in the developing world operate in a very different environment than in the industrialized world. Developing world central bankers are more likely to face economic crises, financial panics, and unsustainably large budget deficits. These factors may make the imposition of an "inflation tax" through unbridled expansion of the money supply more attractive than it is in the industrialized world. While inflation targets in the industrialized world are typically adopted on the grounds that inflation should be a couple percentage points lower, inflation in the developing world should often be hundreds of percentage points lower.

Thus, the case for inflation targeting is stronger in the developing world because the probability that monetary policy will be abused for opportunistic gain is much higher. At the same time, there is also a higher probability that an inflation target, once adopted, could be ignored or cast aside. This may happen against the central bank's will — central bankers in the developing world are more likely to be dismissed or have their desires overridden by the government. And unsustainably large budget deficits may make the use of the printing presses unavoidable, whether the central bank likes it or not.

The effect of inflation targeting on inflation in the developing world is impressive, as seen in Table 8. Inflation rates came down in every developing country that adopted an inflation target, often dramatically. In Brazil and Poland, inflation rates were reduced from triple to single digits, and in Peru, rates were reduced from quadruple to single digits. Nearly every country to adopt an inflation target had a prior history of high inflation (although in some cases, inflation had been reduced to single digits before the imposition of the target.) Inflation rates also became more stable after the adoption of the target, with the exception of Chile and South Korea, the latter of which was severely affected by the Asian crisis.

When compared to the inflationary performance of each country's region from 1995 to 2004, inflation targeters in the Western Hemisphere and Eastern Europe outperformed the region as a whole. There was a secular decline in inflation in these regions as time passed, and the record is less impressive if the comparison is limited to 2000-2004, when inflation averaged 7.8% in the developing Western Hemisphere and 14.5% in the Eastern Europe. The relative performance of targeters is less impressive in newly industrialized Asia (e.g., Thailand, South Korea): inflation was extremely low throughout the entire region in the last ten years. Thailand's rate with an inflation target was slightly lower than the overall region; South Korea's was slightly higher. (The standard deviation of a country cannot be meaningfully compared to the standard deviation of a region, and is not included.)

Since output gaps are not systematically calculated for developing countries, average economic growth rates are used as a proxy. About twice as many countries increased their average growth rate after the target than saw it decline. However, growth rates became less volatile, as measured by their standard deviations, in all countries except Colombia and South Korea, the latter of which was suffering from the Asian crisis at the time it adopted the inflation target. When compared to their region's as a whole, there is no clear correlation between inflation targeting and average growth. As expected, other factors seemed to trump targeting in the determination of average growth, although an inflation target was associated with a more stable business cycle.

As good a record as inflation targeting has in the developing world, it still does not answer the omitted variable bias question — a question that, by its nature, cannot be settled and is posed in starkest terms in the developing world. Many developing countries adopted an inflation target as part of their efforts to break with their profligate past. Brazil, Colombia, the Czech Republic, Guatemala, Peru, Poland, and South Africa had already made major strides to reduce their inflation rates before adopting a target.[45] Clearly, it was political will — particularly to reduce the budget deficit — not the inflation target that was the primary reason for their success. But could they have broken with their past as effectively without a target? Or did the target lock in disciplined behavior, and make back-sliding harder? It is noteworthy that there is not a single country who has abandoned an inflation target yet. By contrast, the fixed exchange rate regimes that many developing countries adopted during currency reforms in the 1980s were often abandoned quickly.

Table 8. Economic Performance of Inflation Targeters (Developing Countries)

Country	Inflation Rate — Average	Inflation Rate — Standard Deviation	Economic Growth — Average	Economic Growth — Standard Deviation
Brazil				
pre-target (1990-1999)	854.8%	1,033.7%	1.8%	2.9%
post-target (2000-2004)	8.7%	5.9%	2.7%	2.0%
Chile				
pre-target (1981-1990)	20.5%	5.8%	3.3%	6.6%
post-target (1991-2000)	9.6%	5.9%	6.5%	3.7%
Colombia				
pre-target (1989-1998)	22.2%	5.4%	2.9%	2.8%
post-target	7.9%	1.9%	1.7%	3.1%
(1999-2004)				
Czech Republic				
pre-target (1993-1997)	11.4%	4.3%	2.3%	2.5%
post-target (1998-2004)	3.7%	3.4%	2.1%	1.8%
Guatemala				
pre-target (1993-2002)	8.6%	3.0%	3.7%	1.0%
post-target (2003-2004)	6.5%	0.8%	2.4%	0.3%
South Korea				
pre-target (1988-1997)	6.2%	1.6%	7.5%	1.8%
post-target (1998-2004)	3.5%	2.1%	4.3%	5.5%
Hungary				
pre-target (1992-2001)	7.4%	1.7%	2.5%	2.7%
post-target (2002-2004)	3.8%	1.5%	3.5%	0.5%
Mexico				
pre-target (1989-1998)	20.8%	8.9%	3.4%	3.4%
post-target (1999-2004)	7.8%	4.7%	2.8%	2.5%

Table 8. Continued

Country	Inflation Rate — Average	Inflation Rate — Standard Deviation	Economic Growth — Average	Economic Growth — Standard Deviation
Peru				
pre-target (1984-1993)	1,252.2%	2,293.0%	0.9%	6.7%
post-target (1994-2003)	7.4%	6.9%	4.3%	4.2%
Phillippines				
pre-target (1993-2002)	16.0%	7.5%	3.6%	1.9%
post-target (2003-2004)	5.8%	1.5%	5.4%	1.0%
Poland				
pre-target (1989-1998)	109.2%	172.5%	2.6%	5.0%
post-target (1999-2004)	4.9%	3.5%	3.3%	1.7%
South Africa				
pre-target (1991-2000)	9.0%	3.2%	1.8%	1.9%
post-target (2001-2004)	5.5%	3.2%	3.2%	0.5%
Thailand				
pre-target (1991-2000)	4.6%	2.2%	4.6%	5.9%
post-target (2001-2004)	1.7%	0.9%	5.1%	2.1%
Turkey				
pre-target (1993-2002)	73.1%	19.7%	3.1%	6.3%
post-target (2003-2004)	18.0%	10.4%	7.0%	1.5%
Memorandum:				
Newly Industrial Asia (1995-2004)	2.5%	—	4.8%	—
Developing Western Hemisphere (1995-2004)	12.2%	—	2.5%	—
Eastern Europe (1995-2004)	25.7%	—	3.8%	—

Source: Author's calculations based on data from Organization of Economic Cooperation and Development, International Monetary Fund.

Notes: Inflation is based on the CPI or RPI index. The post-target period is dated from the first full year that the target is in place. Data covers 10 years before and after (if possible) inflation targeting was in place. Data for the Czech Republic dates back to the country's founding in 1993.

CONCLUSIONS

Overall, there is conclusive evidence that economic performance improved for industrialized countries after the adoption of an explicit inflation target. As expected, inflation fell and became more stable after the adoption of the target, but this improvement did not come at the expense of significant macroeconomic instability as critics claimed it would. However, when compared to similar countries that did not explicitly target inflation, it is not clear that the performance of targeters was superior. One cannot rule out the possibility that good economic performance may have been due to other factors that occurred at the time inflation targeting was introduced.

The evidence suggests that good monetary policy depends above all on the intentions and commitment of the central bank. Whether inflation targeting is a useful way to reinforce that commitment is subject to debate and probably hinges highly on the political institutions particular to each country. Furthermore, the execution of monetary policy under explicit inflation targeting may not appreciably differ from the practice in other countries. Countries without explicit inflation targets like the United States may be implicit inflation targeters, in the sense that there is a widespread perception that the Fed will increase interest rates whenever inflation exceeds 3-4%. Countries that are already implicit inflation targeters may find little difference in performance following the adoption of an explicit target.

Many of the countries surveyed adopted inflation targets in response to the failure of the previous monetary policy regime. Sweden and the United Kingdom adopted targets soon after having their exchange rate forced out of the European Exchange Rate Mechanism (ERM). New Zealand adopted its target after experiencing several years of double digit inflation. Developing countries such as Brazil, South Korea, Turkey, and Thailand adopted targets after experiencing currency devaluation and economic crisis. Under such circumstances, these countries presumably had more to gain from a regime purportedly designed to promote stability and credibility.

If the introduction of an inflation target coincides with disinflationary monetary policy intended to reduce the inflation rate, temporary losses in output and employment are likely to occur. In the five economies surveyed in this report, most or all of the disinflation actually occurred before the inflation target was implemented. The disinflations mostly coincided with the worldwide recessions of the early 1990s, and it is not clear to what extent the disinflations were planned and to what extent they were the byproduct of those recessions. The recessions were brief, and it is difficult to find evidence that the disinflation left negative lasting effects on economic growth, although in some targeting countries average unemployment was higher in the 1990s than 1980s. Since U.S. inflation has been low for over a decade it is unlikely — barring changes in monetary policy — that a disinflationary period would need to accompany the introduction of an inflation target domestically. Thus, the temporary losses in output and employment experienced abroad would not be experienced in the United States and should not be used as an argument against inflation targeting here.

In practice, inflation targets have not taken the pure form that some of their proponents may have envisioned when stressing the regime's purportedly positive effect on transparency, accountability, credibility, and the de-politicization of monetary policy. Exceptions to the target have proven to be the norm and target ranges have been made relatively wide to prevent interest rate and exchange rate instability. Incidents where the inflation rate moved slightly outside the target range have not resulted in abrupt changes in policy. Likewise, target regimes do not live up to opponents' worst fears — central banks under targets have still been willing to use monetary policy to counteract economic slowdowns. At most, one could argue that the targeters caused policymakers to counteract the slowdowns less aggressively than they should have. For example, in the 2001-2002 slowdown, the European Central Bank lowered interest rates more slowly and less aggressively than the Federal Reserve.

Fiscal consolidation occurred in all five of the surveyed economies during the inflation targeting period. This arguably contributed to the targeting regimes' success since it likely reduced inflationary pressures, taking pressure off of monetary policy to meet the targets requirements. In this decade, some or all of the improvement in the budget balance has been reversed for all five of the countries except New Zealand.

The performance of inflation targeting in developing countries is more unambiguously successful. Monetary policy is more likely to be abused in developing countries, so the potential benefits of a regime that "ties the hands" of policymakers is greater. Inflation rates came down in every developing country after the adoption of the target, and targeters outperformed non-targeters in every region except Newly Industrialized Asia. Perhaps the single most important piece of evidence that inflation targeting has been a success in the developing world is the fact that no country has yet abandoned its target.

References

[1] Testimony of Alan Greenspan before the Subcommittee on Domestic Monetary Policy of the Committee on Banking, Finance, and Urban Affairs, 101st Cong., 1st sess., hearing on H.R. 409, Oct.5, 1989, p. 6.

[2] Federal Reserve Reform Act of 1977 (P.L. 95-188).

[3] For a detailed discussion of these issues, see CRS Report 98-16, *The Federal Reserve: Should Its Mandated Goal Be Price Stability? The Issues and Technical Problems*, by Gail Makinen and Marc Labonte.

[4] For an introduction to monetary policy issues, see CRS Report RL30354, *Monetary Policy: Current Policy and Conditions*, by Gail Makinen and Marc Labonte.

[5] See CRS Report RL31056, *Economics of Federal Reserve Independence*, by Marc Labonte.

[6] Statisticians refer to this phenomenon as omitted variable bias: it could be that inflation targeting did not cause responsible monetary policy; rather, responsible policymakers simultaneously pursued low inflation policies and adopted inflation targets. Because there is no way to directly measure responsibility, the improvement is attributed to the inflation target — which is measurable — instead.

[7] For similar overviews, see Edwin Truman, *Inflation Targeting*, Institute for International Economics, (Washington, DC: Oct. 2003); Frederic Mishkin and Klaus Schmidt-Hebbel, "One Decade of Inflation Targeting in the World: What Do We Know and What Do We Need to Know?" *National Bureau of Economic Research (NBER)*, working paper 8397, July 2001; Ben S. Bernanke et al., *Inflation Targeting* (Princeton: Princeton University Press, 1999); Ben S. Bernanke and Frederic S. Mishkin, "Inflation Targeting: A New Framework for Monetary Policy?" *Journal of Economic Perspectives*, vol. 11, no. 2, Spring 1997, pp. 97-117.

[8] It should be noted that low inflation is not an end itself, but a means to an end. There are many ways in which lower and more stable inflation could improve economic efficiency. For example, lower inflation would reduce tax and investment distortions, reduce uncertainty in planning, and divert resources away from the unproductive avoidance of inflation. At the relatively low rates of inflation found in the industrialized world, however, these improvements in efficiency may be too small to translate into measurable increases in GDP growth. Indeed, it is difficult to find such improvements in the data. Thus, this report focuses on whether inflation targeting makes growth more

stable, rather than focusing on whether it increases growth rates. For more information, see CRS Report RL30344, *Inflation: Causes, Costs, and Current Status*, by Marc Labonte and Gail Makinen.

[9] In implementing an inflation target, there was a transition period in many countries when the inflation rate was reduced for a couple of years before it was kept within the long-run target boundaries. This is likely to have caused economic growth and employment to have fallen temporarily. In many countries, part of the disinflation occurred before the announcement of the target regime. Furthermore, in the case studies to follow, this transition period frequently coincided with the widespread economic downturn of 1990-1991, which was partly caused by factors beyond these countries' control, including the oil shock following the Iraqi invasion of Kuwait. Whether the disinflation should be attributed to the pre-target regime (because the need for disinflation came from the policies of the past), the target regime (because policymakers could have left inflation high in the absence of the target to avoid negative GDP effects), or external factors (e.g., the oil shock) is a matter of debate. It can be argued that the transition period should not be included in the target period because it may exaggerate the future costs of the target (once complete, the disinflation would not need to reoccur). Nevertheless, in Table 1, the transition period is included in the post-target period since this was part of the historical cost of the regime. In the individual country studies below, the transition costs are set out separately.

[10] The U.S. and Japan have independent central banks with multiple goals (one of which is price stability), a high degree of policy discretion, and floating currencies. Denmark has maintained a fixed exchange rate since 1982, first with the German mark then with the Euro, which means that its monetary policy is set *de facto* by the ECB. Hong Kong maintains a currency board tied to the U.S. dollar, a form of monetary policy where policy is automatically determined by the number of U.S. dollars entering Hong Kong, giving its central bank very little discretion to change policy. Singapore, has a multiple goal monetary policy, with a greater focus on managing the (floating) exchange rate than U.S. or Japan. Cyprus' monetary policy discretion is limited by an exchange rate that was fixed within a band.

[11] Prices are sticky because of the presence of information costs, uncertainty, contracts, and menu costs. Products with high "menu costs" are those which are costly to re-price. Restaurant menus,

periodicals, and catalog items are examples of products with high menu costs.

[12] Many countries have adopted an inflation target too recently to conclusively judge their track record. In particular, the standard deviation is not a particularly meaningful measure for a data series with only a couple of observations. Thus, although included for all countries, it does not convey particularly useful information for countries who have very recently adopted an inflation target.

[13] One way to allow a central bank to respond to changes in economic activity without breaching the target is to make the target range sufficiently wide that modest changes in inflation are not deemed a concern.

[14] More evidence on the behavior of inflationary expectations can be found in David Johnson, "The Effect of Inflation Targeting on the Behavior of Expected Inflation," *Journal of Monetary Economics*, vol. 49, 2002, p. 1521. He found statistically significant evidence that inflation targeting, all else equal, would bring down expected inflation by about one percentage point the year after its announcement.

[15] Ben S. Bernanke et al., *Inflation Targeting* (Princeton: Princeton University Press, 1999), chap. 10. In their sample, four countries are considered to be inflation targeters: New Zealand, Great Britain, Sweden, and Canada.

[16] See also John Ammer and Richard T. Freeman, "Inflation Targeting in the 1990s: The Experience of New Zealand, Canada, and the United Kingdom," *Journal of Economics and Business*, vol. 47, 1995, pp. 165-192; Bennett T. McCallum, "Inflation Targeting in Canada, New Zealand, Sweden, the United Kingdom, and In General," NBER Working Paper No. 5579, May 1996.

[17] Technically, a government cannot commit future governments to a specified target range. Thus, "indefinite period" must be understood to be until the end of the then sitting parliament. However, it is increasingly the experience that maintaining the target rate is a litmus test for monetary responsibility. Thus, opposition parties during elections pledge to maintain the target if elected. For this reason, the target takes on a life of its own.

[18] For each of the four focus countries, comparisons will be made between the period in which the goal of price stability was fully implemented vs. the same number of years prior to the single goal regime. The transition period, in which the new regime had been announced but the central bank had not yet been required to reach its

ultimate inflation target, is not included in either set of results. Since the 0% to 2% goal was to be reached at the end of 1993, we designate 1994 as the full implementation of the new regime for New Zealand.

[19] Murray Sherwin, "Inflation Targeting — The New Zealand Experience," available at [http://www.bank-banque-canada.ca/publications/conf/con97/cn97-14.pdf], p. 267.

[20] Ideally, the comparison in each period should be the difference between the actual unemployment rate and the "full employment rate of unemployment," the latter of which might vary over the different time periods. In other words, since monetary policy cannot influence the full employment rate of unemployment, the regime should be considered a success if the unemployment rate was kept closer to the full employment rate than in the earlier period, regardless of which period had the lowest unemployment rate. Since the full employment rate is not available for all countries, we present the actual unemployment rate instead as a suggestive measure.

[21] See also OECD, *Economic Surveys: New Zealand*, July 2002.

[22] Joint Statement of Finance Minister and Bank Governor, Feb. 26, 1991.

[23] See also John Ammer and Richard T. Freeman, "Inflation Targeting in the 1990s: The Experience of New Zealand, Canada, and the United Kingdom," *Journal of Economics and Business*, vol. 47, 1995, pp. 165-192; Bennett T. McCallum, "Inflation Targeting in Canada, New Zealand, Sweden, the United Kingdom, and In General," NBER Working Paper No. 5579, May 1996.

[24] Since the Canadians have estimated that the upward bias in their CPI is at most 0.5%, something else must be behind the decision to keep the range at 1% to 3%. It may lie in the fact that some of the Bank's research has shown that this range is sufficiently wide to accommodate control error and unexpected shocks, mainly supply in nature, over and above those due to food, energy, and the first round effects from changes in indirect taxes. We date 1996 as the beginning of the new price stability regime, omitting the transition period.

[25] Ben Fung, Scott Mitnick, and Eli Remolona, "Uncovering Inflation Expectations and Risk Premiums from Internationally Integrated Financial Markets," Bank of Canada working paper 99-6, 1999. This study derived a measure of inflationary expectations based on the yield curve on government bonds.

[26] Agathe Cote, et al, "Inflation Expectations and Real Return Bonds," *Bank of Canada Review,* Summer 1996, p. 40. This study analyzed the

yield on inflation-indexed bonds and consumer surveys on inflationary expectations. Unfortunately, the inflation-indexed bonds were not issued until 1991, so it is not possible to compare if inflationary expectations changed after the inflation target was introduced.

[27] It is interesting to note that the path and goals for inflation announced on Feb. 26, 1991, became embodied and used in the preparation of the government budget. They replaced the inflation forecast that had been used before the Feb. announcement.

[28] The average compound rate of GDP growth between 1996 and 2001 was 3.9% vs. 1.6% between 1986 and 1991.

[29] The contraction in monetary policy actually predated the inflation targeting regime. Short-term interest rates were in double-digits from 1989 to early 1991.

[30] The Chancellor of the Exchequer is the British equivalent of the American Secretary of the Treasury.

[31] See also John Ammer and Richard T. Freeman, "Inflation Targeting in the 1990s: The Experience of New Zealand, Canada, and the United Kingdom," *Journal of Economics and Business*, vol. 47, 1995, pp. 165-192; Bennett T. McCallum, "Inflation Targeting in Canada, New Zealand, Sweden, the United Kingdom, and In General," NBER Working Paper No. 5579, May 1996.

[32] See Ben S. Bernanke et al., *Inflation Targeting*, (Princeton: Princeton University Press, 1999), p. 147.

[33] This index is not compiled by the Bank of England.

[34] The reason for the two-year lag is that current changes in monetary policy are expected to have an effect on the inflation rate only in the future.

[35] Cedric Scholtes, "On Market-Based Measures of Inflation Expectations," *Bank of England Quarterly Bulletin*, Spring 2002, p. 67.

[36] The average compound rate of growth during 1993-2001 was 3.0% vs. 2.4% during the 1984-1992 period.

[37] See also Bank for International Settlements. *Monetary Policy in the Nordic Countries: Experiences Since 1992*, Policy Papers No. 2, Oct. 1997; Bennett T. McCallum, "Inflation Targeting in Canada, New Zealand, Sweden, the United Kingdom, and In General," NBER Working Paper No. 5579, May 1996. For the Riksbank's perspective, see Lars Heikensten, "The Riksbank's Inflation Target — Clarifications and Evaluation," *Sveriges Riksbank Quarterly Review*, 1999:1.

[38] Lars Heikensten, "Inflation Targeting — The Swedish Experience," [http://www.bank-banque-canada.ca/publications/conf/con97/cn97-16.pdf], p. 285.

[39] The average compound rate of growth between 1996-2001 was 3.0% vs. 0.7% over 1987-1992.

[40] The Riksbank *Inflation Reports* can be accessed at [http://www.riksbank.se].

[41] Factual information from this section comes from Otmar Issing et al., *Monetary Policy in the Euro Area* (Cambridge: Cambridge University Press, 2001).

[42] For more information, see Anne Brunila, Marco Buti, and Daniele Franco, eds., *The Stability and Growth Pact*, Palgrave (Hampshire, U.K.: 2001).

[43] M. Forsells and G. Kenny, "The Rationality of Consumers' Inflation Expectations: Survey-Based Evidence for the Euro Area," *European Central Bank working paper 163*, August 2002. The authors derive an estimate of inflationary expectations based on the European Commission Consumer Sentiment survey.

[44] For example, see Hugh Williamson, "Germany to Urge ECB to Cut Interest Rates," *Financial Times*, Oct. 16, 2002, p.5; John Berry, "Euro Still Struggling as Debut of Cash Nears; Challenge to Dollar Fails to Materialize," *Washington Post*, p. D7, Dec. 26, 2001; "Irrational Pessimism," *The Economist*, Dec. 8, 2001; Hamish Mcrae, "Don't Lay All the Blame at Poor Duisenberg's Door," *The Independent*, p. 23, Oct. 20, 2000; Mark Tran, "Growing Pains for European Bank," *The Guardian*, August 30, 2001; Tony Barber, "Anxious Midwife Awaits Birth of the Euro," *Financial Times*, Dec. 19, 2001.

[45] It should be noted that countries which made major strides in reducing their inflation rate over time would have high standard deviation to their inflation rate (e.g., Chile). This would give the misleading perception that their inflation performance had been more unstable than it truly was.

INDEX

A

B

C

D

E

J

K

L

M

N

O

P

R

S

T

U

V

W

Y